NORTHWEST AIRLINES

GEOFF JONES

PLYMOUTH PRESS

First published 1998

ISBN 1-882663-28-4

All rights reserved. No part of this book may be reproduced or transmitted in any form or by any means, electronic or mechanical, including photocopying, recording or by any information storage and retrieval system, without permission from the Publisher in writing.

© Ian Allan Ltd 1998

Co-published by Plymouth Press Ltd and Ian Allan Publishing Ltd.
Distributed in the United States by Plymouth Press Ltd, 101 Panton Road, Vergennes, VT 05491.

For a free catalog of Plymouth Press books and products call (800) 477-2398 or (802) 877-2150.

Printed in Great Britain.

Contents

Introduction	3
Acknowledgements	4
History	5
Strategy	24
Partners	30
Northwest's Hubs	46
Northwest Cargo	58
Training	66
Aircraft	70
Engineering	82
Fleet List	86

Front cover: *Northwest tails at London Gatwick.*
Geoffrey P. Jones

Back cover: *The first RJ35 of Mesaba Airlines, Northwest Jet Airlink entered service in June 1998.*
Norman Pealing Ltd

Right: *Michael E. Levine, Executive Vice President at Northwest Airlines in mid-1998 with responsibility for Marketing and International Affairs.*
Northwest Airlines

Introduction

Northwest Airlines, the main subsidiary of the Northwest Airlines Corporation (NWA Inc), is unassailably the world's fourth largest airline. It is a massive commercial organisation in the air transport world, founded in August 1926 as Northwest Airways, and is America's oldest carrier with continuous name identification.

Northwest Airlines forged the current vogue of airline alliances when, in 1992, it was awarded anti-trust immunity and signed a Commercial Co-operation and Integration Agreement with the Dutch national carrier KLM — Royal Dutch Airlines. This alliance enabled the two airlines to grow and prosper in a far more integrated way than other alliances and code-share agreements that now exist amongst the world's airlines. A further step in expansion and consolidation was taken in January 1998, when Northwest Airlines and Continental Airlines of Houston, Texas (the US's fifth largest airline) announced that they had signed an alliance agreement, to be sealed by Northwest acquiring a 14% equity stake in Continental. The ramifications of this are still under discussion and subject to ratification, but it probably spawned the subsequent rash of other alliances announced between the other major US airlines.

Always centred on the northern US Midwest, Northwest Airlines is headquartered at Minneapolis/St Paul on the border of Minnesota and Wisconsin, also its main hub: the other domestic hubs are at Detroit, Michigan and Memphis, Tennessee, together with two Asian hubs in Tokyo and Osaka. As with most of the US's major airlines, Northwest started life as a mail carrier, and the name Northwest Airlines was adopted in 1934. In 1947 Northwest pioneered the 'Great Circle' route to Asia with services to Tokyo, Seoul, Shanghai and Manila: its strong ties with this market saw the adoption of the name Northwest Orient Airlines in the 1970s and 80s, but this has since been dropped. None the less, Northwest has historically had, and still has, a bigger presence in Asia, particularly Japan, than any other US airline.

Above: *Boeing 747-227B N633US in the airline's old colours (but no longer with 'Northwest Orient', just 'Northwest' branding) taxies at San Francisco in October 1987. This aircraft is one of three ex-Braniff 747s currently in the Northwest fleet.* Tony Carre

The company was reorganised in 1985 to form NWA Inc, a holding company for Northwest Airlines and other subsidiaries. The following year it acquired Minneapolis-based Republic Airlines, but 1989 saw Northwest file for Chapter 11 bankruptcy protection, as the airline struggled against severe competition, declining standards, huge bills for new aircraft and falling passenger numbers and revenue. It took until 1994 to turn itself around, but the following years have seen a resurgent Northwest shake off these problems and become one of the most profitable and respected airlines in the world. Northwest Airlines now boasts, along with its partners, service to more than 400 cities in over 80 countries on six continents. Northwest operates more than 1,700 daily flights in its own right, with more than 130 nonstop flights between the US and Asia each week. It employs more than 50,000 people worldwide and operates a fleet numbering 406 aircraft, with a further 113 on order.

Northwest Airlink is the name used by Northwest Airlines for its network of 'commuter' feeder services by participating carriers Express Airlines 1, Mesaba Airlines and Business Express Airlines. They mainly feed Northwest's hubs at Minneapolis/St Paul, Detroit and Memphis, accounting for more than 400 additional flights per day. Northwest Cargo is one of the world's largest cargo airlines with eight dedicated Boeing 747 freighters.

In 1997 Northwest Airlines' revenue increased to $10,226 million, with a net result (profitability) of $597 million. Load factors increased by 1.2% over 1996's figure to 74.3%, and the guideline of all US airlines, revenue passenger kilometres (RPK), increased from 1996's figure by 4.9% to 115,898 million.

Northwest Airlines is not just a US institution but a worldwide one, more so since the alliance with KLM, and still further following the tie-up with Continental. Other alliances have been forged, so that Northwest and KLM, together with their 29 respective airline partners, operate 60,000 code-share flights per month. This book aims to give a brief, yet comprehensive overview of the major areas of Northwest Airlines' operations and services. Information is current to early July 1998, but in the rapidly changing world of air transport, is subject to change and alteration without notice. Further up-to-date information can be obtained by accessing Northwest's website at: www.nwa.com.

Above: *Northwest took delivery in May 1968 of the 707th Boeing 707 built, a 707-320C convertible cargo-passenger version. This airline publicity shot shows Boeing employees saluting the landmark delivery with a more austerely dressed Northwest flightcrew.*
Geoffrey P. Jones collection

Acknowledgements

The author would like to thank many employees at Northwest Airlines in both London and Minneapolis/St Paul, particularly Doug Killian and Susan Maring at the International Communications Department in Minneapolis/St Paul, for their help in providing much of the information in this book. Thanks are also due to photographers who have helped fill several of the gaps in the author's own collection, notably Sara Steig at Northwest Airlines, D. S. Osborne and Tony Carre.

History

Above: *Original Northwest Airways logo from the 1920s.*
Geoffrey P. Jones collection

It was Michigan-based businessman Col Louis H. Brittin who in 1926 saw the potential in the US Midwest of the Contract Air Mail or CAM routes. These were established following the passing of the 1926 Kelly Act for the carriage and delivery of US Mail between major commercial centres. He raised the necessary capital, some of it from Henry Ford and a Detroit consortium, and successfully bid for CAM 9, the route between Chicago and the Twin Cities (Minneapolis/St Paul). He then formed Northwest Airways in August 1926, and flew the first air mail service from the Twin Cities to Chicago under the CAM 9 contract on 1 October 1926.

Because much of the new airline's backing was from the state of Michigan, the company was registered as a Michigan company, but with an operational base in the Twin Cities. A rented Thomas Morse Scout and Curtiss Oriole were the first two aircraft used by Northwest Airways, the legendary stunt and air racing ace Charlie 'Speed' Holman was its first pilot, and Louis Brittin the Vice President and General Manager. Northwest Airways operated its flights from the Speedway Field in the southern outskirts of the Twin Cities, a former motor-racing track turned airfield that later became known as Wold Chamberlain Field.

Northwest quickly realised the potential of an air service carrying not just the CAM 9 mail but passengers as well. Northwest, along with Florida Airways, became the launch customer of the newly formed, Detroit-based Stinson Aircraft Corporation, buying the first of four of their new enclosed-cabin, single-engined biplanes, Stinson SB-1 Detroiters, at $12,500 per aircraft. On 5 July 1927, local St Paul businessman Byron Webster was press-ganged by Brittin into becoming Northwest's first official ticketed passenger. Flown by Holman, the eventful first passenger flight to Chicago turned into a 12.5hr adventure, routeing via La Crosse,

Wisconsin, Madison, Wisconsin, Milwaukee and hence to Chicago where they landed in darkness at 02.30 on 6 July.

Demand wasn't great for the $40 single fare flight to Chicago: by the end of 1927, 106 passengers had been flown safely on the route by Northwest Airways. Weather was always a problem, with rain, storms, winds, snow and fog, but 88.9% of their published schedules were completed in the first three months of operations (122 total trips), a typical Twin Cities-Chicago flight taking 4hr 40min and the return a longer 5hr 5min. The service was terminated for the harsh Minnesota winter.

In 1928 Brittin established a Northwest flight school, a sightseeing service over the Twin Cities, a dealership for Waco biplanes and a revolutionary air-rail service for mail and passengers. By 1929 Northwest Airways was flying two routes between the Twin Cities and Chicago, one on the original route via La Crosse, Madison and Milwaukee, the other via Rochester, Minnesota. It also started a new service from Chicago along the western shore of Lake Michigan, using Stinson Detroiters and calling at Milwaukee, Fond du Lac, Oshkosh, Appleton and Green Bay. Other aircraft were added to the Northwest fleet: Waco biplanes, of course; Hamilton Metalplanes, the first of eight; and most revolutionary for the time with seats for 14 passengers, the first of five Ford 5-AT-C Trimotors, delivered new to Northwest Airways at the Twin Cities on 31 August 1928 and costing $65,000 (registered NC7416). The Trimotors were used to open up the most prestigious Northwest Airways air-rail service, with passengers travelling from the Twin Cities to Chicago by air and then transferring to the train for the onward journey to New York. The additional capacity brought to the Twin Cities-Chicago route led Northwest to cut its fares in order to fill its extra seats. At $30 single and $50 return the airline was able to compete with first-class rail fares.

February 1928 saw Northwest fly the first international service to Winnipeg, Canada, although this was short-lived. With the Ford Trimotors, expansion of the airline's route structure became a practicality.

Below: *Laird LC-B 'Commercial' outside Northwest's original wooden hangar at Wold Chamberlain Field in 1926 with the airline's first pilot, the notorious Charles 'Speed' Holman in the white flying suit. Geoffrey P. Jones collection*

Left: *Hamilton H-45 Metalplane introduced by Northwest Airways in 1928. By 1934 the airline had eight in its fleet.*
Geoffrey P. Jones collection

Right: *Travel Air 6000 NC9933 of Northwest Airways, one of four purchased in 1931. Note the AM9 (Air Mail route No 9) designation alongside the company logo.*
Northwest Airlines

During the early 1930s, links between the Twin Cities and the Lake Michigan townships were strengthened and new routes forged, southwest from the Twin Cities to Sioux City and Omaha and northwest to Fargo (North Dakota) and Winnipeg. These were the first days of airline alliances, over 60 years before the Northwest/KLM alliance. The old Northwest Airways placed great emphasis on its links with other airlines for connecting passenger flights at both Chicago and Omaha; and also with the railway companies, again at Chicago but also in Winnipeg. In 1931, services commenced to Duluth, at the western tip of Lake Superior: as the city didn't have an airport, Northwest purchased two eight-passenger Sikorsky S-38 amphibians for the service from the Twin Cities, using the harbour at Duluth for landing. Conventional services also started to Elgin and Rockford, Illinois.

Northwest Airways 'came home' on 1 July 1930 when it was purchased by a group of Minnesota financiers. They also moved the airline's headquarters from Wold Chamberlain Field to the St Paul Downtown Airport on the banks of the Mississippi River. Northwest pilots, particularly 'Speed' Holman, had been conducting survey flights for possible new routes, all the time trying to push west towards the Rockies. By 1932, Northwest's route map extended as far west as Jamestown and Bismarck, North Dakota. A route through to Seattle and the Pacific was the ultimate aim. In the bleak weather conditions of the northern Midwest winter, Northwest Airways gained huge experience of dealing with the problems such conditions created, and many of their aircraft were retro-fitted with skis for winter operations. Other aircraft types operated by the airline at this time included several Travel Air 6000s, Laird LC-R200

Above: *One of two Sikorsky S-38 amphibians bought by Northwest Airways in 1931 to serve Duluth, which had no airport at the time.*
Northwest Airlines

Below: *Ford 5-AT-C Trimotor, NC8410 with the Northwest Airways logo prominent on the rear fuselage, one of five owned by the airline from 1928 until the mid-1930s.* Northwest Airlines

Speedwings, Stinson SM-2AB Juniors and various Waco biplanes, including the Waco Model 10 and J-CTO.

March 1933 saw further route expansion to Billings, Montana via Glendive and later that year as far west as Missoula. On 23 October, Northwest started serving Spokane (on the eastern border of Washington state) and on the historic day of 3 December the goal, Seattle, Washington. Tacoma was added the following day. Northwest's Northern Transcontinental line was established, and, with 'special advisers' Amelia Earhart and Charles Lindbergh on the first flight, the publicity and euphoria was tremendous. Thanks to Northwest Airways, US transcontinental air services had become a reality. Three Lockheed Orions joined the airline's fleet prior to the delivery of the first Lockheed 10 in 1934.

February 1934 saw the US government take control of the US Air Mail contracts and pass them wholesale to the US Army Air Corps. Brittin took great exception to this and other government intervention in the airline industry, and resigned from Northwest Airways. Shreeve Archer took over as President and the new Minnesota-based owners reincorporated the airline as Northwest Airlines Inc on 20 April 1934.

Despite these hiccups, the airline industry was fast on the road to further expansion, and Northwest Airlines became the first to fly the Lockheed 10A, its fleet eventually totalling 13 10As and one 10B. By 1937, Northwest, which had worked diligently with Lockheed over a specification for a larger version of the Lockheed 10, took delivery of its first 14-passenger Lockheed 14H 'Sky Zephyr', able to fly the prestigious Minneapolis/St Paul to Chicago route in 1hr 45min and the Chicago-Seattle route in 10hr 15min. The same year Croil Hunter took over as President. There would eventually be 29 Lockheeds in the Northwest fleet. Northwest was not the quickest off the mark to order the 'new' Douglas DC-3. The route structure and passenger loads didn't demand them, and the Lockheed Sky Zephyrs were quite adequate. However, Northwest was not to be left behind: it managed to sell the airline's 10 remaining Sky Zephyrs at the same price they were purchased for two years earlier, and the order for six DC-3s costing $110,000 each didn't frighten their accountants too much.

The DC-3's arrival was also the start of the era of the airborne stewardess or flight attendant, Northwest hiring its first two in 1939 — Virginia Johnson in Minneapolis and Dorothy Stump in Chicago. By the time of Pearl Harbor in December 1941, Northwest Airlines had 11 DC-3s in its fleet, with four more on order, but with four Lockheed 10s still giving sterling service. Passenger numbers had risen dramatically since 1934:

Year	Passengers Carried
1934	12,097
1935	25,123
1936	38,022
1937	37,786
1938	46,323
1939	74,519
1940	136,797
1941	149,212

Northwest Airlines' war effort was unrivalled. The workforce jumped from 881 to over 10,000. Half of its fleet was requisitioned by the US Army Air Force, but it was Northwest's experience and expertise at cold-weather flying that led to its assignment to open up an air-bridge to Alaska, as Japan had captured several of the Aleutian Islands and was threatening mainland Alaska itself. Using its own DC-3s plus USAAF Curtiss C-46s and Douglas C-47s, it plied the northwest route across the Yukon from Seattle and from Minneapolis to Anchorage, Fairbanks, Fort Yukon and Nome carrying troops, supplies, equipment and food. Northwest crews flew a total of 21,559,469 miles on Alaskan missions, carried 44,977,183 ton-miles of cargo and amassed 164,814,621 passenger miles.

Northwest's other major contributions to the war effort were 10 special war projects, most significant of which was its Bomber Modification Center. At Holman Field, St Paul and at Vandalia, Ohio it carried out

Above: *Lockheed Orion at Grand Central Air Terminal, Glendale, Los Angeles. Northwest added these six-passenger, 205mph airliners to its fleet in 1934.*
Geoffrey P. Jones collection

specialist modifications to B-24 Liberators, B-25 Mitchells and B-26 Marauders, at one stage employing over 6,000 at St Paul: 3,286 bombers were outfitted or modified by Northwest during the war.

On 1 June 1945, Northwest Airlines achieved one of its major milestones and ambitions when it flew a DC-3 on its first coast-to-coast transcontinental US flight from New York to Seattle. 1945's passenger total almost doubled its prewar figure, at 330,489, and Northwest Airlines was well and truly back in business. Wartime experience in Alaska put Northwest in an excellent position for its first DC-4 Seattle to Anchorage flight in September 1946. This was part of a new goal: authority to fly the Great Circle route to the Orient. On 15 July 1947, the DC-4 N95418 flew the first of a three-times-a-week schedule from Minneapolis/St Paul on the Northwest passage via Alaska to Tokyo, Seoul, Shanghai and Manila, the elapsed time for the Minneapolis/St Paul to Tokyo flight being 36hr 35min against a flight time of 33hr 5min. This was the start of a growing association between Northwest Airlines and the countries of east and southeast Asia that has remained one of the airline's strengths right up to 1998.

In 1947, Northwest ordered 10 Boeing 377 Stratocruisers and the first 10 of what was to be a 25-aircraft fleet of Martin 202s. The 202s replaced the DC-3s, starting in 1948, and introduced another of the airline's traditional identities, the red tail: the stylised compass logo was also introduced in 1947-8. The first of the Stratocruisers was introduced in 1949, bringing new standards of passenger comfort and service to Northwest's long-haul services, including those to Tokyo, cutting eight hours off the flight time of the older DC-4s. The Martin 202s were a disappointment and were all sold by 1952. New aircraft were ordered: 24 DC-6s entered service in 1954, and six Lockheed Super Constellations were ordered in 1953 for service entry in 1955. DC-7Cs followed in 1957. The Constellations were soon sold to finance purchase of more DC-6s.

1954 was the end of an era at Northwest Airlines, as Croil Hunter was replaced as President by Donald Nyrop. He inherited a somewhat financially troubled airline, refinancing the huge new aircraft debts and orders. New routes were needed, and Northwest applied for services to Los Angeles, San Francisco and Miami. In another early example of airline alliances,

Above: Fourteen-seat 14-H 'Sky Zephyr', built by Lockheed to a Northwest Airlines specification as a larger replacement for its Lockheed 10s. Introduced in 1937. Northwest Airlines

Northwest reached agreement with Eastern Air Lines for an interchange agreement, using its Stratocruisers in winter and Eastern's Constellations in summer. Northwest crews flew the Minneapolis/St Paul to Chicago sector and Eastern crews took over for the onward flight to Miami. Also in 1955 Northwest was granted rights to fly Chicago-New York together with the right to stop at Detroit.

Still flying from Holman Field at St Paul, despite occasional flooding from the Mississippi, Northwest's first Lockheed L188 Electras arrived in 1958 while the airline waited for the delivery of its first jet aircraft and a move to Wold Chamberlain Field. Northwest still had 24 DC-6s and 17 DC-7Cs in service, but the first of five Douglas DC-8s arrived in 1960, earmarked for the trans-Pacific routes to the Orient. Following these in July 1961 was the first of 17 Boeing 720s used first on the flagship Minneapolis/St Paul-Chicago-New York route, and in December 1962 on the New York-Honolulu route (via Chicago-Seattle-Portland). Although it entered service with PanAm in 1958, Northwest didn't receive its first Boeing 707, a 707-320, until 1963 — the first of an eventual fleet total of 41 aircraft, and at the time representing the biggest ever order for a single aircraft type in the airline's history. Several of the 707s were in a 'combi' configuration, permitting the carriage of mixed passenger/cargo loads.

With the advent of jets came the long overdue move from Holman Field at St Paul to the comparatively huge Wold Chamberlain Field in 1960. This is still the main base and hub of Northwest Airlines. The cities of Minneapolis and St Paul adopted the airport as the Twin Cities Airport and in January 1962 opened a new $10 million jet-age air terminal. With Northwest rapidly establishing its operational, administrative and maintenance base here, many innovations were achieved, including the first centralised domestic radio communications system of any US trunk airline. Northwest also supported and pioneered many research projects to assist the rapidly growing domestic US commercial aviation industry, such as research on clear air turbulence, aircraft noise reduction and weather research.

The 1950s had been uncertain years both financially and operationally, but this all changed in the 1960s when Northwest Airlines turned in incredible growth along with increasing profitability. Although only the seventh largest US airline in 1968 and

Above: *Northwest Airlines did not take delivery of its first Douglas DC-3 until 1939, several years later than many contemporary US airlines. NC21715, seen here at Minneapolis airport, was one of 11 DC-3s the airline operated until the time of Pearl Harbor in 1941.* Geoffrey P. Jones collection

1969, Northwest's profits (at over $50 million) were greater in both years than any other of the top seven airlines. 1964's figures were boosted by the Olympic Games in Tokyo and a large increase in Northwest traffic.

While the Boeing 720s and 707s had been used for domestic flights, the era of the true domestic jet service started for Northwest in 1964 when the first three Boeing 727-100s entered service. By 1966 Northwest Airlines had an all-jet fleet of 61 aircraft, and had 20 more on order, plus an order for its first 10 Boeing 747 'Jumbo Jets'. Building work on new maintenance facilities to house these huge new jets also commenced at Wold Chamberlain Field. Although the airline had been using the epithet Northwest Orient Airlines on advertising and some written material since

Left: *Used by Northwest Airlines between 1940 and 1942 for route survey flights and training, a Cessna T-50 'Bobcat'.* Geoffrey P. Jones collection

Left: *Northwest Airlines Douglas DC-4, introduced in 1945. One of 41 flown by the airline in the 1940s and 1950s, the aircraft is seen at Wold Chamberlain Field, c1947.*
Geoffrey P. Jones collection

1950, its strengths in serving the Orient had grown to such an extent that it was decided to officially call the airline Northwest Orient Airlines. The first aircraft so branded was one of 19 new Boeing 727-200s. With the first 747s, long-haul routes were developing, including several to or via Hawaii as Northwest strengthened its position in the Californian market. The first Northwest Orient Airlines 747 schedule was flown on 22 June 1970 between Minneapolis/St Paul and New York, and soon after it became the first airline to offer 747 services across the Pacific from the four major gateways of Seattle, San Francisco, Los Angeles and Honolulu. Five longer-range 747Bs or 747-200s were added in 1971. Standardisation was also paying off at Northwest with an all-Boeing fleet: the 707, two types of 727 and the 747, all with Pratt & Whitney engines.
A proposed merger between Northeast Airlines and Northwest in 1969 failed at the last moment, and Delta Air Lines took over Northeast. Another merger nearly happened in 1970 between Northwest and National Airlines.

Donald Nyrop surprised the airline industry, and Boeing, in 1971 by ordering 14 Douglas DC-10-40s. The surprise was not only in the breakaway from Boeing, but more significantly that the DC-10s would be fitted with Pratt & Whitney JT9D engines, as fitted to Northwest's 747s, rather than General Electric engines. As a result, these DC-10-40s could carry 236 passengers an additional 1,205 miles further than standard DC-10s. The first Northwest DC-10s entered service in November 1972.

In 1973 Northwest aircraft landed at Peking (Beijing) for the first time since 1949, and by the end of 1974 all 22 of Northwest's order for DC-10s had entered service.

Right: *As a DC-3 replacement, the Martin 202 was introduced in 1948 with an order for 25 aircraft. They were all sold by 1952. N93051 is shown with a Washington DC background.*
Northwest Airlines

Above: *With routes to the Orient being flown by DC-4s, the delivery of the first of 10 luxurious Boeing 377 Stratocruisers in 1949 cut eight hours off the flight time to Tokyo. Here the 25th anniversary of the first Northwest air mail flight is being celebrated in 1951 with an early Waco biplane and Stratocruiser 'New York' at Minneapolis.* Geoffrey P. Jones collection

On the airline's 50th birthday in 1976, Donald Nyrop resigned the presidency and Joe Lapensky took over. It also celebrated the birthday with continued profitability ($43.2 million). The all-jet aircraft fleet totalled 113 aircraft, including the first three of the eight all-freight 747-200Fs it had on order:

Type	Fleet size	Capacity
Boeing 747	17	369 passengers
DC-10-40	22	236 passengers
Boeing 707-320	8	165 passengers
Boeing 727-100	32	93 passengers
Boeing 727-200	31	128 passengers
Boeing 747-200F	3	105 tons of cargo

When the Airline Deregulation Act became law in October 1978, few airlines fully appreciated what impact it would have on US domestic services. Its effects, although not immediate, were compounded in 1979 by a doubling in jet fuel prices, fuel now representing 42% of the airline's costs and with the US economy sliding into recession.

1979 saw Northwest start a whole range of new domestic services such as Philadelphia-Fort Lauderdale and Boston-Orlando, spurred by the competition of deregulation. It also made its first foray into Europe, firstly with cargo flights from Boston and New York to Glasgow on 9 February, followed on 31 March by the first transatlantic passenger service from Minneapolis/St Paul via Detroit and New York to Copenhagen and Stockholm. Passenger service to Glasgow followed on 28 April and on 2 June 1980 the first Minneapolis/St Paul to London Gatwick schedule commenced. Northwest Airlines has had a continuous presence at Gatwick ever since. Boeing 747s were used on these flights. The fight to obtain rights to fly Minneapolis/St Paul to London was not an easy one, with 15 cities (along with several airlines) competing to be the one new US gateway that was up for grabs under a new US/UK air rights treaty. Four airlines (Braniff, World, Capitol International and Northwest) were also competing at the time for rights to fly from Boston to London. Northwest won, and flew the first service on 26 April 1981, with onward service to Hamburg.

Above: *Northwest ordered Lockheed L-1049 Super Constellations in 1953, the prototype first flew on 12 December 1954 and they entered service in the spring of 1955, known as the 'Super G'. N8201 is seen here on an early test flight over the greater Los Angeles conurbation.* Northwest Airlines

Steven Rothmeier became President and Chief Operating Officer in September 1983, and soon after became responsible for Northwest's biggest airliner order ever, valued at $2 billion, for 10 of the new Boeing 747-400s, 10 Boeing 757-235s and three Boeing 747-200s. Reflecting its new global structure, the company also officially dropped the word Orient from its advertising and titling, again becoming simply Northwest Airlines.

Continental Airlines, now a partner of Northwest, filed for Chapter 11 bankruptcy protection in September 1983, only surviving with a dramatic slim-down of employees and routes, and by becoming de-unionised. It was a bad time for US airlines: the Civil Aeronautics Board (CAB) had lost control over route licensing and fares by the end of 1982, and the effects of growing competition following deregulation were compounded by a weak US economy. Competition grew on international routes, so that Northwest was joined at London Gatwick by other new-comers Delta, Braniff, Western, Air Florida, Capitol International and People Express.

In 1984 a new corporate identity was established, with Northwest Airlines operating as a wholly owned subsidiary of NWA Inc: future expansion and business diversification were the reasons for this. Computerisation was already an important element of running an airline of Northwest's size and diversity, and in the early 1980s $55 million was spent, particularly for more efficient fares and ticketing availability. A marketing agreement with Mesaba Airlines was signed in 1984, and it became the first Northwest Airlink operator. The first two of the Boeing 757-251s arrived in March 1985, heralding the start of Boeing 727 disposals and another new era of greatly improved efficiency in the domestic market.

Competition at Minneapolis/St Paul had increased dramatically, mainly due to the growth of Republic Airlines, also based alongside Northwest in the Twin Cities. In October 1986, Northwest acquired DC-9 operator Republic Airlines, more than doubling its aircraft fleet and stifling most of the cut-throat competition on its home patch.

Republic Airlines

Republic was founded as Wisconsin Central Airlines in Clintonville, Wisconsin in 1946. It used a 'flying duck' logo from day one, right through to the 1986 takeover. In 1952, under its new President Hal Carr, it changed both name and headquarters, becoming North Central Airways and moving to Minneapolis/St Paul. The route network grew from a modest 19 Midwest destinations to an almost nationwide network stretching from Denver to New York by the time of deregulation. A merger with Atlanta-based Southern Airways on 1 July 1979 brought the name change to Republic Airlines.

Several west coast local service airlines including West Coast, Empire, Zimerly, Southwest and Bonanza eventually merged in 1968 to form Air West and then soon after, with investment from Howard Hughes, Hughes Air West in 1970.

One common thread through Southern, North Central and Hughes was that they were all DC-9 operators. Hughes then merged with Republic in 1980 as the new airline filled another geographic gap in its growing nationwide route network. Flying to 107 US cities with a 168-aircraft fleet, including 126 DC-9s, the airline had hubs at Minneapolis/St Paul, Detroit and Memphis. It was a difficult time for Republic, with high interest rates, the first deliveries of an order for Boeing 757s and continuing intense competition post-deregulation. After nearly a year of negotiations between Northwest's Rothmeier and Republic's Stephen Wolf, Northwest agreed to buy Republic for $884 million in a cash-for-stock deal.

This merger catapulted the newly enlarged Northwest Airlines from the seventh to the fourth largest US airline.

Below: *Flying over Waikiki, Honolulu in the 1950s, one of 24 DC-6s operated by Northwest from 1954 onwards. The word 'Orient' appears in the airline's name for the first time on the lower tail.* Geoffrey P. Jones collection

Below: *Fast, pressurised and comfortable, the Douglas DC-7C helped Northwest transition from the prop to the jet era, first entering service in 1957.*
Northwest Airlines

On 8 June 1989, Northwest became the first US airline to take delivery of the Airbus Industrie A320, having placed an order for 50 in 1986 with options on a further 50. A speculative order for Airbus A340s was also placed in 1988, but subsequently cancelled. Northwest also became the launch customer for the Boeing 747-400 and operated the type's first international passenger flight on 1 June 1989 between New York and Tokyo.

Profitability had always been a keyword at Northwest, but the large aircraft orders, the Republic merger costs, post-deregulation competition and costly worldwide expansion had negative effects. Although the airline returned a $73.2 million profit on an operating revenue of $2,655 million in 1985, the slide was underway.

1989 was the disaster year. Northwest Airlines filed for Chapter 11 bankruptcy protection, its problems compounded further by the huge bills for new aircraft, declining standards, falling passenger numbers and hence dramatically reduced revenue. Restructuring was made possible when Northwest Airlines became privately owned in a $3.65 billion transaction by a group of investors known as Wings Holdings, headed by Alfred Checchi, Gary Wilson and Fred Malek. NWA Inc was now a privately-held company, for the first time since 1941.

The climb back to success and profitability started, and in January 1990 a $422 million programme was announced to upgrade service and build customer relations. John H. Dasburg was named President and CEO of NWA Inc in November 1990, and he retains this position in 1998. By the end of 1990, Northwest had the best on-time performance of the seven largest US airlines.

Northwest and KLM's joint flights from Amsterdam to Minneapolis/St Paul started on 2 April 1991, and at the end of the year claimed its position for best on-time performance, retaining it in 1992, 1993, 1994 and 1995. 1992 was a consolidation year, the overstretched expansion of former years turning to rationalisation. Northwest started to withdraw to the core areas it

Above: *With the Imperial Eagle on the all-red tail of this Lockheed Electra, and small Northwest Orient Airlines titling near the nose, the links the airline had established with trans-Pacific destinations were already well established by 1959.* Northwest Airlines

knew best, those likely to be more profitable. The mini-hubs it had created at Washington National (DC) and Milwaukee were closed, the Seoul, Korea hub was dramatically downsized, and services to Australia were abandoned so that the airline could concentrate on developing its Japanese hubs and focus. With the Northwest/KLM alliance blossoming, non-strategic transatlantic routes were suspended to allow more transatlantic flying from main US hubs, particularly Detroit, and also from Amsterdam. On 11 January 1993 the US Department of Transportation approved the Northwest/KLM Commercial Co-operation and Integration Agreement with the grant of anti-trust immunity. This was a world first, enabling the creation of the first unified global airline system, described in detail later. By March, Northwest and KLM had begun an expansion of code-sharing to more than 30 Northwest destinations in North America and more than 30 KLM destinations in Europe, the Middle East and Africa. On 7 December 1993, Wings Holdings, the parent corporation of Northwest, was renamed Northwest Airlines Corporation.

World Business Class was introduced in February 1994 and was another joint development by Northwest and KLM. The decision was also taken in 1994 to carry out major hush-kitting and refurbishment of the DC-9-30 fleet. International services and passenger numbers to Asia also grew, with new services from Detroit to both Osaka and Tokyo, and by November 1994 its one millionth Japanese passenger of the year had boarded, reaching this milestone much earlier than ever before. A marketing and code-share agreement between Korea and the US was also signed with Asiana. The gloom of Chapter 11 and the unprofitability of the early 1990s was now history, as sound management and an increase in staff morale and efficiency were paying off.

Above: *First jet aircraft to fly with Northwest was the Douglas DC-8C, the first of five arriving in 1960 and earmarked for services to the Orient. N802US is seen here during its inaugural visit to Tokyo.* Northwest Airlines

Below: *DC-8C N804US fresh from the Douglas Long Beach factory prior to delivery to Northwest Airlines in 1961.* Geoffrey P. Jones collection

Above: *In December 1962, Northwest Airlines started flying Boeing 720s on its New York to Honolulu route via Chicago, Seattle and Portland. The first of 17 were delivered in July 1961. N721US is seen against the backdrop of Waikiki, Honolulu.* Northwest Airlines

1994 saw the red ink disappear from the Northwest balance sheet, as the airline returned a $295.5 million net profit, the best of any US major airline for that year. The days of the nickname 'Northworst' were now over, and passengers and the media were happy to call the Minneapolis/St Paul-based airline 'Northbest'!

In 1996, Northwest's traffic totalled 110,440 million revenue passenger kilometres: in contrast top US airline,

Above: *Three Northwest Airlines Boeing 720Bs, along with four Eastern Air Lines 720s on Boeing's pre-delivery flight line at Seattle in 1962. (N728US in the foreground is still without its port outer engine.)* Geoffrey P. Jones collection

Above: *Celebrations of Northwest's 50th anniversary in 1976 were enhanced by the arrival at Minneapolis/St Paul of a Stinson Junior and Waco biplane owned by Daniel F. Neuman, one of its Boeing 747 captains. The aircraft were painted in original Northwest Airways colours, although these particular aircraft didn't actually fly with Northwest in the 1920s and early 1930s they were representative of types that did. DC-10-40 N155US, delivered new in December 1973, provides scale and contrast.* Northwest Airlines

United's corresponding figure was 187,765 million. Expressed as actual passengers carried, Northwest's total was 32.682 million, compared to Delta, which carried the most at 97.281 million. Northwest was also the world's fourth most profitable airline in 1996 behind British Airways, American and Singapore Airlines. In terms of total sales, Northwest ranked eighth in the world.

These exceptional figures helped Northwest's celebrations in 1997 of the 50th anniversary of the start of its trans-Pacific services. On 15 July 1997, in a ceremony at Minneapolis/St Paul, a DC-4 specially painted in Northwest's 1940s livery was parked next to a 747-200. This celebration involved every aircraft in the Northwest fleet, all carrying the '50 Years — Bridging the Pacific' logo. The ultimate celebration of the first DC-4 flight from the Twin Cities via Anchorage, Shemya (Alaskan Aleutian Islands), Tokyo, Seoul, Shanghai and Manila was the painting of Northwest's

Left: *As part of the July 1997 celebrations of the 50th anniversary of Northwest's scheduled services to the Orient with DC-4s, the airline loaned the Berlin Airlift Historical Foundation's C-54 Skymaster N500EJ painted in its original 1947 livery. It is seen at Minneapolis/St Paul with Boeing 747-227B N635US.* Northwest Airlines

'World Plane', Boeing 747-400 N670US adorned with award-winning artwork created by children from the US and Asia.

On 19 August 1998 Northwest further enhanced its services to the Orient when it made the first scheduled commercial flight using one of the new routeings across the North Pole and Siberia with one of its Boeing 747-400s. It was on a scheduled Detroit-Beijing flight, using the Polar 2 Route which takes the aircraft within 100km (55nm) of the North Pole and knocked 45min off the normal scheduled flight time on this service, which formerly operated via Alaskan and northern Pacific airspace.

Above: *Northwest Orient Boeing 747-251B N613US, landing against a classic oriental backdrop and wearing the colours adopted from the mid-1960s until the late 1980s.* Northwest Airlines

Below: *Just prior to the 1986 takeover of Republic, the airline changed its livery and started taking delivery of six Boeing 757-2S7s (including N602RC here). These flew with Northwest for a while, but were sold to America West Airlines.* Geoffrey P. Jones collection

Above: *The first Boeing 747-151 delivered to Northwest in April 1970, N601US. It will soon be retired, with the two other 747-151s.* Boeing

Above: *A familiar sight at London Gatwick in the 1980s after Northwest Orient commenced transatlantic services from Minneapolis/St Paul. This aircraft is a 747-151, N608US, one of only three early-model 747 'classics' still in the Northwest fleet in 1998, and shortly to be withdrawn from service.* Tony Carre

Strategy

An assessment by with Mike Levine, Executive Vice President — Marketing & International Affairs of Northwest Airlines, June 1998 (see photo Page 2)

Most airlines have strategies or business plans for their future development. Interacting with these plans are changes in the airline environment. Most significant of these in recent years has been affiliations, mergers and alliances. The affiliation between Northwest and Continental has been on the screen for a long time. Many of Northwest's senior executives and investors know their equivalents at Continental quite well; in particular Northwest's principal shareholder, David Bonderman, Northwest's CEO John Dasburg and Continental's CEO Gordon Bethune who all meet regularly at airline regulatory gatherings and airline functions. It's all down to figuring out how to survive in the cut-throat airline business and how to make money for the airline's shareholders.

A Continental/KLM alliance didn't fit. Gary Wilson and Al Checchi, Chairman and Co-Chairman of Northwest headed the group of investors who bought out Northwest in the 1989 privatisation of the airline and returned the company to the public stock market in 1994. They had built up and strengthened the airline's influence in the US's north-western states, through the alliance with Seattle-based Horizon Air, which had become part of the Alaska Air Group in 1986. The recent alliance between Northwest and Alaska Airlines was therefore almost inevitable: it was considered to be worth trying to strengthen the Northwest influence in this part of the US, to cement the already strong relationship between the two groups, but without any equity or shareholding of one airline in the other. There is no single or simple recipe for success in such an alliance.

It was partly this success within the US — excluding the partnership between Northwest and KLM — that helped define the deal with Continental in late 1997 and early 1998, which is a financial agreement

Above: *With downtown Minneapolis as a backdrop, Northwest Airlines DC-9-31 (in the old colour scheme) and Boeing 757-251 (in the new scheme) are on final approach to land on the parallel runways 11R and 11L in this 1995 view.*
Geoffrey P. Jones

Above: *Douglas DC-9-31 N920RW (Fleet No 9960) at the jetway on 'E' Concourse at Detroit in June 1997.* Geoffrey P. Jones

plus an alliance. Northwest feels that what it did influenced the other US majors, prompting the United Airlines/Delta Air Lines tie-up proposal and the American Airlines/US Airways tie-up, but personally Mike Levine doesn't think it's obvious how commercially serious these proposals are. Politically both Northwest and Continental prefer the situation where the two airlines are smaller, because if they were larger there is more likelihood of intervention by government agencies.

Northwest and Continental have actually signed a contract which will give Northwest a 14% equity stake in Continental, although Continental will remain totally independent. Code-sharing was not going to take place either, until the somewhat tricky labour contract negotiations of summer 1998 with its pilots and other maintenance staff had been concluded. Because there is a financial agreement involved, it is subject to the Hart/Scott/Rodino approval from the US Department of Justice. There are three tracks which the deal has to address: maximum co-ordination without government intervention, the Hart/Scott/Rodino approval and approval from various governments for the joint venture because of the bilateral alliance between Northwest and KLM.

No problems to any of these three aspects are anticipated and the discussions over new contracts with pilots' unions should be resolved amicably. In principle, Levine considers that the pilots are perfectly willing to settle, it's just the terms and conditions that need resolution. (Settlement was reached but regrettably after strike action.

Northwest's strong position in Asia has been affected by the economic problems in southeast Asia. Its plans to serve Indonesia have been shelved, but they will start service to Malaysia as planned. There is a substantial and large Asian market and although in 1998 this is a bit soft, it's a great economy which can be restructured to perform overall and shouldn't be written off. Northwest took up a defensive posture as a result of the economic malaise, but as 10% of Japan's international traffic is flown by Northwest, it has to remain positive and retain its presence.

The alliance signed between Northwest and Air China in May 1998 and the discussions with Thai Airways International for a similar deal are evidence of Northwest's strong hold on the Asian region. In fact Air China is the first Chinese airline to enter an international alliance, and the deal is also more all-embracing, being a strategic alliance between Air China and Northwest, as well as Continental, Alaska and America West. The Sino-US Bilateral Air Services Agreement allows the two carriers to code-share on up to five destinations, likely to be on Northwest's five nonstop services between Beijing and Northwest's Detroit hub. Levine anticipates considerable growth in the Chinese market provided the country remains politically stable, and he also expects the Korean economy to bounce back very soon. The current economic difficulties are the subject of repair work rather than wholesale restructuring, and this is illustrated by the Philippines, where the market is now holding up better than anticipated.

The European market gives grounds for optimism, particularly with the announcement of the start of Italian/US bilateral air negotiations and the establishment of an 'open skies' agreement. Alitalia has signed an alliance with KLM, which in turn allows full co-operation with KLM's US partners, Northwest and Continental. This four-way joint venture is certainly not of the size of the similar Star Alliance airline grouping, but is of major significance to the development of a global system that will help to make profits for Northwest and its other three partners. Levine believes that the Star Alliance is broader but not as 'deep' as Northwest's grouping and pointed to the alleged anomaly that had transpired on joint Lufthansa/United flights, with totally diverse pricing structures on the same seats on the same flights. Northwest has ensured that any commercial differences between the airlines are settled first — it also believes that big isn't necessarily beautiful, preferring the current smaller four-airline alliance.

Below: *Departing from Minneapolis/St Paul runway 10L in June 1998, one of the newest Boeing 757-251 aircraft in the Northwest fleet, N547US (one of the original order for 48 aircraft).* Geoffrey P. Jones

Northwest doesn't have any magic recipe to remain profitable. It continually assesses its market, trying to remain flexible in a disciplined way. More than any other business, it takes pride in the organisation and doing what its customers want.

Expansion and development of Northwest has taken place in the Asian/Chinese market and also now in India. The airline's planners do not, however, wake up in the morning and look at a world map to see which areas are not yet coloured red and then try to develop new routes and markets in these areas. Northwest, like any other airline, is providing travel facilities to the general public for 365 days a year. It used to run the same schedule all year round, but now has become more flexible and, listening to what people want, responded to fluctuating markets. An example of this is the blend between business and leisure travellers. Northwest now flies many flights just at the weekend: for example, there are 15 destinations served in Mexico and the Caribbean from Minneapolis just on a Saturday. Leisure flights are often run in conjunction with a sister NWA Inc tour company, MLT. Among many other such services are those to ski destinations in the Rockies in the winter.

Northwest isn't afraid to take risks and look for new opportunities. For example, it was the first US airline to serve the new Osaka (Kansai) airport when every other airline was holding back. This airport serves a region of Japan with a population of 25 million, and Northwest's early presence here is now paying rich dividends. There are also markets that Northwest is not interested in, such as the low-cost, short-haul, point-to-point services of airlines such as Southwest and Delta Express. Northwest prefers its hub-and-spoke operations from three major US hubs, plus its development of international services to Asia and Europe.

Fleet development goes hand-in-hand with routes and markets. Northwest has established something of a niche for itself

Below: *Acquired by Northwest following the 1986 takeover of Republic Airlines, Boeing 727-251 N721RW (c/n 21200) was originally a Hughes Airwest aircraft. Seen here at Detroit in October 1987, in the hybrid colour scheme adopted by Northwest for ex-Republic aircraft, this aircraft is no longer in the Northwest fleet.*
Tony Carre

Partners

KLM

KLM uk

Continental Airlines

eurowings

Garuda Indonesia

JAS

AIR NEW ZEALAND

Post-deregulation (1978) the US airline industry reeled under the shock of severe competition, both on fares and new upstart airlines. Established airlines, including Northwest, had to go with the flow or find themselves on the scrapheap. While much of Northwest's international network, particularly to Asia and Europe, was unaffected, its domestic network came under considerable pressure. For example, in 1978 there were nine airlines serving Minneapolis/St Paul carrying 11 million passengers annually with 220,000 aircraft movements: by 1985 there were 33 airlines carrying exactly the same number of passengers but needing 330,000 aircraft movements.

December 1984 saw Northwest take an important step along the way to securing its domestic viability with the establishment of its first Airlink franchise and code-share with Mesaba Airlines. This in particular helped safeguard its main base at Minneapolis/St Paul. By 1981, local competitor Republic had a fleet of 180 aircraft compared to only 120 in the Northwest fleet. Northwest regarded Minneapolis/St Paul as a hub, one of the many that the post-deregulation era spawned.

Northwest's President and CEO of the time, Steven G. Rothmeier, explained its strategy: 'We are expanding and strengthening working relationships with regional airlines serving important Northwest hub airports. We have entered into an advanced marketing agreement with Mesaba Airlines, a dominant regional (commuter) carrier serving Minneapolis/St Paul. Under this new system, Mesaba will operate as a Northwest Orient Airlink, and every Mesaba flight will be designated a Northwest flight number. The benefits to travellers are closely co-ordinated flight schedules between the two airlines and a full range of competitive fares.' (Northwest was called Northwest Orient at this time.)

Left: Northwest MD-82 and Boeing 757 at Minneapolis/St Paul in June 1998 together with three of Mesaba's Northwest Jet Airlink RJ85s.
Geoffrey P. Jones

The Airlink deal was designed to turn Mesaba's network into a feeder system for Northwest's longer-haul flights from Minneapolis/St Paul. The PR slogan at the time was 'a two-airline connecting service with one-airline convenience'. Scheduling and ticketing were merged, so that a passenger could have just one ticket from the small cities that Mesaba served right through to any of Northwest's domestic destinations, or even international destinations such as London or Tokyo.

Mesaba Airlines

Mesaba Airlines celebrated its 25th anniversary of scheduled flying in 1998, and two of its new Saab 340Bs have been painted in special commemorative liveries to celebrate the anniversary.

It is a typical regional airline, one of thousands worldwide that collectively carry an estimated 70 million passengers a year and are growing at around 6% a year. The company was incorporated in January 1966 as a division of Halvorson Inc, based at Grand Rapids, Minnesota and offering flight training, charters and air ambulance services. Scheduled air services started on 4 February 1973, and in 1977 Mesaba Aviation was purchased by the Swenson family. By 1980, the airline operated a Cessna 421B Golden Eagle and a Beechcraft 99 on twice-daily commuter services between Grand Rapids and Minneapolis/St Paul and from Minneapolis/St Paul to Alexandria, Detroit Lakes and Thief River Falls, all in rural Minnesota. Post deregulation, Mesaba entered into an Essential Air Service agreement and expanded its commuter network from Minneapolis/St Paul to further destinations in Minnesota and also South Dakota, North Dakota and Iowa. A short-lived partnership with Republic Airlines in 1983 was followed by the 1 December 1984 signature of the Northwest Airlink agreement.

At this time Mesaba's fleet comprised turboprop Beechcraft 99s and Fokker F27 Friendships. By the end of the 1980s, Swearingen SA227AC Metro IIIs had replaced the Beech 99s and were an important element of the airline's fleet until 1998, when the last SA227AC was phased out of service. Alongside the SA227ACs (16 in the fleet in 1990), more F27s were acquired (15 in the fleet in 1990) and these remained in service until 1996. Further expansion of Mesaba's fleet and network of Northwest Airlink services occurred in 1992 when the first of 25 De Havilland Canada DHC-8-102As were delivered. In 1994, Mesaba acquired commuter airline Conquest Airlines of Austin, Texas and its SA227 Metro III aeroplanes, and developed it into a Boeing 737-200 jet operator known as AirTran Airways, and based at Fort Lauderdale, Florida. This was spun-off in 1995, coinciding with Northwest Airlines taking a 29.7% financial stake in Mesaba. It was at this time that Mesaba Airlines' current CEO, Bryan Bedford joined the airline.

Development of Northwest's other major northern US hub at Detroit saw a diversification of Mesaba's activities and growth of their presence here, with code-shared Northwest Airlink feeder services alongside Northwest's other major Airlink partner Express Airlines 1. This saw an interchange of aircraft between Mesaba and Express and between Northwest's three US hubs at Minneapolis/St Paul, Detroit and Memphis. Express Jetstreams and Saab 340s are used on Mesaba services from Minneapolis/St Paul, this exchange becoming common with the phasing out of F27 aircraft by Mesaba from 1996. However, in March 1996 Mesaba made a commitment to Saab to acquire nine used Saab 340s of its own: this was subsequently modified to apply to new aircraft as well as used and brought its eventual Saab 340 fleet to 72 aircraft. Nineteen of the new Saab 340Bs will be delivered between February and December 1998, as well as three used Saab 340As. Mesaba's DHC-8 fleet is currently being phased out.

Parent organisation of Mesaba Airlines and Mesaba Aviation in 1998 is Mesaba Holdings, with the Chairman of the Board Carl Pohlad and the President and CEO Bryan Bedford. 1,700 employees work for Mesaba Airlines, the airline serving 87 destinations throughout 17 US states and Canada, of which 41 destinations are served nonstop from Minneapolis/St Paul. 1996's net income at Mesaba was $12 million, rising to $19.6 million in 1997. Projections for 1998 and 1999 are $19.8 million and $24.3 million, as average sector lengths flown by regional airlines are increasing: 192 miles in 1992 and currently 234 miles.

Apart from Northwest's purchase of an equity stake in Mesaba Airlines, mainline Northwest also ordered 12 Avro RJ85s in October 1996 for use by its Airlink partner. Options on a further 24 were also placed. Its RJ85 fleet would then total 36 aircraft.

The move to jet aircraft saw the establishment of a new operation, Northwest Jet Airlink, the RJ85s being sub-leased to Mesaba or Northwest Jet Airlink by the parent, mainline airline. First RJ85 was delivered to Mesaba in late April 1997 and entered service the following month, replacing Douglas DC-9-10s being flown on 'thinner' Northwest routes from both Minneapolis/St Paul and Detroit. In July 1997 Northwest Airlines exercised its options for the further 24 RJ85s in a $620 million order, the largest ever for the RJ85, on behalf of Mesaba. These were to be delivered from May 1998 until 2001, although this was modified in June 1998 to delivery between January 1999 and August 2000. The RJ85 normally has seating for up to 85 passengers, but Mesaba and Northwest have configured their aircraft in a 69-seat layout. This permits a small forward section with two-plus-two abreast business class seating (former DC-9-10 customers were used to this), and it gives more seat-pitch room in coach, but also meets Northwest's scope-clause agreement with its pilots. It is no secret that Northwest pilots were unhappy about the out-sourcing of regional jet flying to Mesaba.

In October 1997, the Mesaba/Northwest code-sharing partnership was extended for a further 10 years. This also gave Mesaba the exclusive rights to operate all connecting flights for Northwest Airlines at both Detroit and Minneapolis/St Paul. 1997's segmented net revenue for Mesaba Airlines was $214 million and 1.7 million passengers were flown. (Segmented revenue means the portion of an origin/destination pair that includes Airlink travel.) 73% of Mesaba/Express passengers connect on to a Northwest mainline flight. Since Bryan Bedford's arrival, on-time departures at Mesaba have improved dramatically to 96%, excluding delays caused by factors over which it has no control. Mesaba Airlines in June 1998 flew to 91 cities in 19 US states and Canada from both Minneapolis/St Paul and Detroit using a fleet of 82 turboprop and jet aircraft.

Above: *A pair of Mesaba Airlines Swearingen SA227AC Metro IIIs at Minneapolis/St Paul in Northwest Airlink colours in June 1995, N26906 nearest the camera. Mesaba had a fleet of 22 Metros, but they had nearly all been phased out of service by June 1998.* Geoffrey P. Jones

Above: *Northwest Airlink Fokker F27 Friendship 200 operated by Mesaba Airlines at Minneapolis/St Paul in June 1995 when Mesaba had nine of the type in its fleet.* Geoffrey P. Jones

Northwest Airlines signed two more agreements in July 1985, with Phoenix Sky Harbour-based America West and Big Sky Airlines of Billings, Montana. Big Sky, initially with HP Jetstreams and then Swearingen Metros, provided connections at Billings, Great Falls and Spokane. Other similar Airlink agreements soon followed. Galion, Ohio-based Fisher Brothers Air Services joined Airlink in February 1986: it operated Short SD360, CASA Aviocar and Dornier Do228 aeroplanes to connect five cities in Ohio and Michigan to Detroit and Cleveland. Marquette, Michigan-based Simmons airlines used Short 360 and ATR42 aeroplanes for services centred on Detroit and Minneapolis/St Paul. Another short-lived Airlink signing was California-based Pacific Southwest Airlines.

The America West agreement was signed on 1 July 1985, and enabled any America West passenger flying into Albuquerque, New Mexico or Burbank and Ontario (John Wayne/Orange County), California to have direct access onward on one of Northwest's flights from these three airports to either of its hubs at Minneapolis/St Paul or Detroit. Passengers on America West flights from its Phoenix hub to Los Angeles International (LAX) could also connect with Northwest's extensive trans-Pacific flight network or its flights to Hawaii. This agreement was seen as a way of enhancing both airlines' competitive positions, and despite America West's difficulties in 1993/94, when it entered and emerged from Chapter 11 bankruptcy protection, this is an alliance that continues in 1998 between Northwest Airlines and what is now the US's ninth largest airline.

Big Sky Airlines signed its Airlink agreement with Northwest on 15 July 1985, in a natural progression of Northwest's presence in Montana since 1933. With a small fleet of seven Cessna 402Cs and Swearingen SA226TC Metro IIs (it had earlier flown Jetstreams), Big Sky flew to 10 cities, including Billings and Helena, served already by Northwest. Big Sky's flights were integrated into Northwest's computer reservation system and were given Northwest flight numbers. This agreement was terminated in 1989 when Big Sky Airlines filed for Chapter 11 bankruptcy, although it did subsequently emerge and continues to fly, albeit on a smaller scale and with no formal links with Northwest.

Below: *Two BAe Jetstream 31s of Express Airlines 1 in Northwest Airlink colours at Minneapolis/St Paul in June 1995. Part of a 21-aircraft fleet at the time, these now operate mainly to Northwest's Memphis hub.* Geoffrey P. Jones

Express Airlines 1

Express Airlines 1 was established in February 1985 and started operations on 31 May, with its head office located in Atlanta, Georgia. Under the Express name, Phoenix Airline Services Inc provided co-ordinated services with Northwest Airlines as an Airlink carrier at both Memphis and its Minneapolis/St Paul hubs. However, the signing of the agreement with Mesaba meant that Express Airlines 1 concentrated on Memphis, although not exclusively. It quickly established a large route network and placed orders for BAe Jetstream 31s and Saab 340As. By 1987, Express Airlines 1, as a Northwest Airlink operator, was providing scheduled commuter-type services from Memphis to 20 destinations in the southern US and from Minneapolis/St Paul to 16 destinations in the Midwest, including Chicago (Midway), Green Bay and Sioux City. It used a fleet of 30 Jetstream 31s and 11 Saab 340As. By 1992, Express also had a small hub operation at Milwaukee, and was serving 40 cities in 15 states with a fleet of 25 Jetstreams and 17 Saab 340s. Three years later, the fleet had increased with the addition of 11 higher-performance Saab 340Bs, now with services to 52 cities in 22 states.

Since the very early days of the airline, Michael J. Brady and his family have been the 100% shareholders, and he continues as its President and CEO in 1998. 1,500 employees currently work for Express, including 430 aircrew and 175 engineering staff.

Express Airlines 1 was put under great pressure during late 1997 to make a commitment on orders for larger aircraft and also for jet aircraft as it started the phase-out of its Jetstream 31s. Northwest Airlines has no equity stake in Express, but could follow the precedent of Mesaba, buying new aircraft and leasing them to Express. Saab 2000s have been considered, along with Bombardier Canadair Regional Jets, the RJ85 and the Embraer EMB-145. No decision had been made by August 1998.

In 1997 Express Airlines 1 accounted for segmented net revenue of $227 million (segmented revenue, as explained earlier, means the portion of an origin/destination pair that includes Airlink travel, so on a Duluth- Minneapolis/St Paul-Los Angeles flight, the revenue from the Duluth-Minneapolis/St Paul portion flown on Airlink counts). Approximately three million passengers flew on Express in 1997 and for Express and Mesaba, 73% of their passengers connected to a Northwest mainline flight.

Northwest Airlines' alliance with KLM Royal Dutch Airlines has been the envy of the air transport world. It was made possible following Northwest's privatisation in 1989. Subsequently the two airlines were granted anti-trust immunity by the US Department of Transportation in January 1993, enabling them to operate their transatlantic flights as a joint-venture alliance in relation to pricing, scheduling, product development and marketing. This was far beyond the usual and more common airline code-share agreements. As a consequence, Amsterdam is effectively another Northwest hub, KLM having promoted and built up its presence over the last 10 years with feeder traffic, particularly from British provincial passengers, formerly with Air UK and KLM City Hopper but now KLMuk. The Northwest/KLM alliance has increased what might have been a moderate 5% per annum growth in traffic to a phenomenal 15%. At an operational level, in pricing, marketing and ticketing, the alliance is very healthy, with customer awareness of the joint operations and passenger benefits throughout both airline networks being more and more recognised and regarded.

This alliance, however, has not been without its problems, and in 1997, KLM, which owned 18.8% of the voting equity in Northwest, wanted to increase its investment to 25%.

Above: *A Saab 340A of Express Airlines 1 in 'old' Northwest Airlink colours at Minneapolis/St Paul in June 1995. This aircraft has now been transferred to the Mesaba Airlines fleet.* Geoffrey P. Jones

Below: *Shortly after the takeover of Republic by Northwest, several commuter airlines were also adopted as Northwest Airlink operators, including Simmons Airlines of Marquette, Michigan. It used Short 360, ATR-42, EMB-110 and NAMC YS-11 aircraft to link into Minneapolis/St Paul, Detroit and Cleveland. Short 360 Adv N384MQ in Northwest Airlink colours is one of its aircraft seen here at Detroit in October 1987.* Tony Carre

Above: *Saab 340A N322PX being marshalled to its parking spot at Minneapolis/St Paul in June 1995. Then with Express Airlines 1, it is now flying with Mesaba as N41XJ.* Geoffrey P. Jones

Below: *Newly delivered to Northwest Airlink carrier Mesaba Airlines in 1998, Saab 340B N439XJ features a special livery to celebrate the airline's 25th year of scheduled services. It depicts the extensive route network centred on the hubs of Minneapolis/St Paul and Detroit.* Geoffrey P. Jones

Boardroom difficulties resulted, partly due to Northwest's fear that KLM was trying to gain control of the US airline — KLM responded with the threat of legal action. This was resolved in August 1997, when KLM agreed to sell its stock in Northwest, and Northwest committed itself to an alliance with KLM for 13 years in an 'enhanced alliance agreement'. Leo M. van Wijk, President and CEO of KLM, remains as one of the Northwest Board of Directors. A formal Northwest/KLM global joint-venture agreement was signed on 29 September 1997, believed at the time to represent the longest and most extensive airline partnership.

This was a springboard for an even stronger alliance, expanding co-operation on passenger services, linking of sales operations, an alliance on cargo services, integrated training, and, perhaps most importantly, the agreement to explore the inclusion of further partners, most notably the Italian national airline Alitalia. This plan materialised in December 1997 when it was announced that KLM and Alitalia had agreed to form a strategic commercial alliance. With Alitalia's hubs at Milan and Rome complementing the KLM hub at Amsterdam, it was felt that this would enhance both passenger and cargo traffic of Northwest, KLM and Alitalia across the Atlantic and within the rest of their extensive route networks. KLM and Alitalia serve 400 destinations in 80 countries and operate more than 60,000 code-share flights a month.

Part of the alliance agreement between KLM and Alitalia was to allow full co-operation on a US/Italian open-skies agreement so that KLM's existing partner, Northwest (and now Continental) was able to co-operate as well. The main obstacle to open-skies agreements is the European Commission, which wants to negotiate directly with the US for a Europe-wide agreement rather than to have separate country agreements.

October 1997 saw Northwest's European partner, KLM, announce its intention to take a 30% stake in the Norwegian airline, Braathens SAFE. Joint maintenance work on

Below: *Seen above a waiting DC-9, Northwest Airlines Boeing 727-2M7 N729RW landing at Minneapolis/St Paul in June 1995. It is an ex-Hughes Airwest and Republic aircraft still operational in the fleet.* Geoffrey P. Jones

Above: *Mesaba Airlines now has one of the biggest Saab 340 fleets in the world, this Saab 340B N414XJ being one of 72 of the 'A' and 'B' models in its fleet by early 1998. This is now being supplemented by orders for and delivery of a further 22 new and used 340s.* Geoffrey P. Jones

their fleets of Boeing 737s started soon after, and the effect for Northwest is additional feed into its network from Scandinavia, mainly via KLM's Amsterdam hub.

The most significant alliance for Northwest, after KLM, was announced on 26 January 1998. Northwest Airlines agreed a long-term commercial alliance with Houston, Texas-based Continental Airlines. Continental is the US's fifth largest airline. Northwest, in a separate agreement, was to acquire a 14% equity stake in Continental, although the management of Northwest have vigorously stressed that there are no plans to merge the two airlines. Instead the alliance will be on similar lines to that with KLM, and the one between Northwest and Alaska Airlines. This includes code-sharing, frequent-flyer scheme reciprocity, co-operation between Continental and KLM, and in particular, as the route networks of the two airlines hardly overlap, greater flexibility and scope on ease of ticketing, check-in and luggage handling on routes for their customers. The two airlines' international customers will also benefit significantly, Continental's from Northwest's Asian strengths and Northwest's from Continental's Latin American strengths.

It is important to look at this alliance in the context of others in the air transport industry. The proposed British Airways/American Airlines alliance had still not been agreed by mid-1998, and in a wider context, the Star Alliance (Lufthansa, United Airlines, Scandinavian Airlines System, Varig, Air Canada and Thai Airways International) is geographically comprehensive but by no means as deep. Delta Air Lines had been talking to Continental, but more along the lines of a merger. Since the announcement of the Northwest/Continental alliance, Delta Air Lines has indicated that it hopes to establish an alliance with United Airlines, although this plan has now been shelved. In this situation Delta would either have to side with United and its other Star Alliance partners, or dismiss such a deal with United and strengthen the partnership it has already established with Swissair, Sabena and Austrian Airlines. American Airlines revealed on 23 April 1998 that it had struck an initial deal with US Airways so that the 'Big Six' US airlines may end up in alliance agreements as the 'Big Three':

Northwest Airlines/Continental Airlines
American Airlines/US Airways
United Airlines/Delta Air Lines

One airline analyst described the Northwest/Continental combination as: 'the cleanest fit — Northwest's strengths lie in its fortress hub at Minneapolis, the well

Above: *In a break with tradition, Mesaba Airlines' RJ85 fleet has been purchased by Northwest Airlines and leased back to Mesaba to operate its Northwest Jet Airlink services. N502XJ and N512XJ are seen here at Minneapolis/St Paul in June 1998: they are taking over some of the 'thinner' Northwest services previously flown by Douglas DC-9-15s.* Geoffrey P. Jones

Below: *Still wearing the 'old' 1970s/80s colours is McDonnell Douglas MD-82 N931MC, Fleet No 9304, at Minneapolis/St Paul in June 1995. It was originally delivered to Republic in 1982 and operated by Muse Air for a while before returning to Republic and then Northwest.* Geoffrey P. Jones

Above: *N148US is one of Northwest's Pratt & Whitney JT-9D-powered Douglas DC-10-40s, rotating for take-off at Minneapolis/St Paul in June 1998.*
Geoffrey P. Jones

Left: *With Northwest and Northwest Airlink dominating traffic at Detroit, more than two-thirds of the 1,500 aircraft operations per day are accounted for by Northwest.* Geoffrey P. Jones

developed trans-Atlantic link with KLM and its privileges on Pacific-Japan routes. The resurgent Continental offers its base in the southern states and a strong presence at trans-Atlantic gateway New York (Newark), as well as a serious challenge to American Airlines' domination of traffic to Latin America.'

Northwest has another Northwest Airlink alliance with the largest regional carrier in the northeast US, Business Express, or BEX for short. Based at Dover, New Hampshire and with a fleet of Saab 340As and Bs, BEX is also a Delta Connection and American Connection carrier as well as a Northwest Airlink carrier. It has over 340 daily departures from its hubs at New York (Kennedy), Boston Logan and New York (LaGuardia): the Northwest Airlink element of BEX is the feed it provides from 14 points in New England and Canada into its Boston hub, flights which link with mainline Northwest Airlines flights to Seattle, Minneapolis/St Paul, Memphis and Detroit.

Seattle/Tacoma-based Horizon Airlines is now a wholly owned subsidiary of the Alaska Air Group, which operates as Alaska Airlines and an official Northwest Affiliate carrier. Horizon was founded by Milton Kuolt in 1981 and flew its first service between Seattle and Yakima, Washington State with two leased Fairchild F27s. Acquiring Air Oregon in 1982, the airline grew rapidly. Horizon became part of the Alaska Air Group in November 1986. It had an intensive feeder network into the two northwestern US cities, Seattle/Tacoma and Portland using DHC-8s, F28 Fellowships and SA227AC Metro IIIs. Early in 1989, both Alaska Airlines and Horizon Air established a code-sharing agreement with Northwest Airlines, retained ever since. Horizon now operates as a Northwest Airlines Service Partner or Affiliate carrier for many of its flights, which then link to Northwest's flights from Seattle to Tokyo, Nagoya and Osaka. Horizon flies a varied fleet, the DHC-8 (both 100 and 200 series) being its mainstay alongside Fokker F28 Mk 4000s. Its Dornier 328-110s are being returned to the manufacturer.

Horizon's 'affiliate' status with Northwest is different to partners such as Mesaba and Express that actually carry the Northwest Airlink brand. The Northwest/Horizon relationship is a code-share agreement that

Below: *Douglas DC-10-40 N144JC, taxying at Detroit in June 1997, was originally N144US until sold by Northwest to the Minneapolis/St Paul-based Sun Country Airlines, re-registered and subsequently leased back to Northwest.*
Geoffrey P. Jones

includes the allocation of revenue for passengers that connect between the two airlines. Northwest doesn't put its NW flight numbers on local Horizon flights, and doesn't have any equity in Horizon.

Northwest's alliance with Alaska Airlines is also as a Northwest Airlines Service Partner, an arrangement similar to that with Horizon, complementing both airlines' services. Alaska is particularly strong in its north-south services along the whole US western seaboard, from Alaska south to California and Mexico. Also in the west, Trans States Airlines operates Northwest Airlink services between Sacramento, San Francisco, Monterey, Fresno, Santa Barbara, Los Angeles (LAX), Ontario, Palm Springs and San Diego.

Northwest Airlines' strength in the Pacific region is further enhanced by Service Partners in Hawaii, Hawaiian Airlines, and in Guam in the Northern Mariana Islands, Pacific Island Aviation. In the Indian subcontinent, the first alliance has been forged by KLM on its own and Northwest's behalf with Boeing 737-equipped domestic airline, Jet Airways of Bombay.

The most recent Northwest alliance, and the first by a US airline with any Chinese airline, was signed in New York on 12 May 1998 between Northwest Airlines, joined by its three other major alliance partners (Continental/KLM/Alitalia) and Air China. Air China has established itself as one of the nation's leading airlines, China's only flag carrier and currently its largest airline. This alliance will provide a basis for operational and marketing alliances between the Northwest Group airlines and Air China, drawing particularly on Northwest's track record in Asia over 51 years. Simultaneously Continental, Alaska Airlines and America West Airlines entered into their own alliance agreements with Air China. Northwest Airlines currently operates a direct Detroit-Beijing service five times a week, and provides the only nonstop flights by a US airline between North America and China. Northwest also provides service to Beijing and Shanghai via Tokyo's Narita airport.

Alliances and partnerships that Northwest Airlines has with other airlines worldwide at a variety of different levels are (as at August 1998):

Air China, Alaska Airlines, Alitalia, America West Airlines, Asiana Airlines, Braathens SAFE, Business Express (BEX), Continental Airlines, COPA (Panama), Emery Worldwide, Eurowings, Express Airlines 1, Garuda Indonesia, Hawaiian Airlines, Japan Air System, Jet Airways, KLM Royal Dutch Airlines, KLMexel, KLMuk, Mesaba Airlines, Pacific Island Aviation, Singapore Airlines and Trans States Airlines.

In June 1998 KLM announced its new alliance with Malaysian Airlines (MAS), a significant extension of the Northwest /Continental/KLM/Alitalia global alliance. A further new code-share agreement between Northwest and KLMexel was signed in August 1998.

Right: *Boeing 757-2S7 N604RC (c/n 23566), on approach to Miami in March 1987, was one of four delivered to Republic in 1985 just before the 1986 merger with Northwest. It was subsequently sold on to America West in September 1987 and re-registered N904AW.*
Geoffrey P. Jones

Left: *Wearing the 'bowling shoe' Northwest livery first adopted in 1989 for Airbus A320 deliveries, Boeing 757-251 N519US at Minneapolis/St Paul in June 1998..* Geoffrey P. Jones

Below: *Boeing 727, DC-9, A320 and DC-10 aircraft of Northwest at Minneapolis/St Paul, Gold Concourse during an afternoon 'bank' in June 1995. There are up to eight banks a day, when waves of aircraft feed into and out of the MSP hub.* Geoffrey P. Jones

Above: At Minneapolis/St Paul in June 1995, BAe Jetstream 31s of Northwest Airlink franchisee Express Airlines 1 in both old (nearest camera) and new liveries. A mainline Northwest Boeing 757-251 taxies past. Geoffrey P. Jones

Below: As it is the world's 14th largest airport in terms of passenger numbers, the domination by aircraft in Northwest colours is understandable, as Northwest accounts for over 1000 flights per day at Detroit. This view looks northeast over 'E' and 'F' Concourses. Northwest Airlines

Northwest's Hubs

After the near disaster of 1989 when Northwest Airlines filed for bankruptcy protection, part of the recovery plan was for the airline to retrench. In the run-in to 1989, Northwest, like several other major US carriers, tried to counter competition by expansion. It didn't work.

Since the 1986 acquisition of Republic Airlines, also based at Minneapolis/St Paul, Northwest Airlines had a strength that it could capitalise on — its almost unchallenged presence and level of service from its Midwest stronghold. Detroit was another important base, and with the airline's presence at Memphis also increased, these three domestic hub operations were the solid base on which Northwest Airlines was able to climb out of its 1989 problems, helped also by the airline's acquisition by a group of private investors headed by Alfred Checchi, Gary Wilson and Fred Malek.

Northwest wasn't just a US domestic airline, though. Its trans-Pacific pedigree started in 1947 with the first Great Circle scheduled passenger service from MSP via Anchorage and Shemya, Alaska to Tokyo, Seoul, Shanghai and Manila. The airline gradually developed the prominence and importance of its two Japanese hubs at Tokyo (now Narita) and at Osaka.

Northwest also had significant links to Europe, inaugurated in March 1979 with the airline's first trans-Atlantic passenger service from MSP, Detroit and New York to Stockholm and Copenhagen. Boston to London Gatwick services commenced on 26 April 1981 and since these dates Northwest's trans-Atlantic services have grown. This culminated in the 1993 grant of anti-trust immunity to Northwest and KLM by the US government, enabling the alliance between the two airlines to become a model for other major carriers. The result shows the importance to both KLM and Northwest of the Amsterdam hub, not just in a European context, but in a transcontinental context, as it feeds into Asia, to Africa and the countries of the former Soviet Union.

Around 85% of Northwest's total traffic in 1994 was into and out of its core areas (the three US hubs, plus Tokyo Narita and Kansai). With Amsterdam added, this has increased to 98%.

Below: *Boeing 727s mingle with DC-10s at Northwest's gates around the Red Concourse at Minneapolis/St Paul in June 1995. The 727-225 aircraft in the foreground, N801EA, is one of nine ex-Eastern Air Lines 727s currently in the Northwest fleet.* Geoffrey P. Jones

Northwest's Major Hubs

Minneapolis/St Paul International
 (The Twin Cities) (MSP)
Detroit Metropolitan/Wayne County
 International (DTW)
Memphis International (MEM)
Tokyo/Narita International (NRT)
Osaka/Kansai International (KIX)
Amsterdam/Schipol International (AMS)

Minneapolis/St Paul

From a small pre-World War 1 concrete race track, Wold Chamberlain Field has become one of the world's major international airports, Minneapolis/St Paul International airport (MSP) handling more than 25 million passengers a year. While the number of aircraft movements has not increased dramatically in recent years, approaching 400,000 per annum, the number of passengers using MSP has increased steadily from 4.8 million in 1985, to 19.2 million in 1990 and to nearly 29 million in 1997. MSP is now ranked 14th among the US's leading airports.

With 11 major airlines using MSP (excluding regional/commuter/cargo/charter airlines), Northwest Airlines is by far and away the most significant, accounting for nearly 80% of total passengers boarding. Northwest has been flying from the Twin Cities since the day of the formation of Northwest Airways in 1926.

In 1997, MSP was ranked 18th largest airport in the world for passenger traffic, at 29.612 million passengers. In 1998 Northwest Airlines accounts for 492 daily aircraft departures from MSP, 339 of them jet services with mainline Northwest and the other 153 Northwest Airlink flights by Mesaba and Express 1.

1997 saw Northwest Airlines respond to the extension and strengthening of the main MSP runway, so that a fully loaded 747 or DC-10 can now depart from MSP direct to Tokyo. In October 1997, Northwest inaugurated a three-times-a-week MSP-Hong Kong service and daily flights to Osaka, and increased the frequency of its Tokyo flights to daily. In connection with KLM, Northwest increased its services eastbound, starting a twice-daily MSP-Amsterdam flight.

Northwest and Northwest Airlink operate from all of the four main terminals at MSP. International flights now depart and arrive at Gates 1 to 9 on Gold Concourse: Gold has a total of 21 gates. The dominance of Northwest here is demonstrated by the Waco J-6, a restored original in the air-mail colours of 1928 Northwest Airways Inc, hanging from the roof alongside the entrances to Gates 11 and 12. Red Concourse's 17 gates are dominated by Northwest, and five gates of Blue and 17 gates of Green Concourses, which are shared with the other airlines using MSP, are dedicated to Northwest use. A major extension of the Green Concourse to handle much of the Northwest Airlink traffic is nearing completion in 1998.

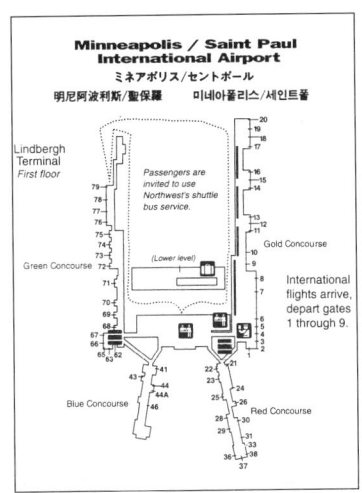

Above: Digitally displayed information for aircraft captains (seen at Gates D10 and D12 at Detroit in June 1997) is an aid to on-time departures. At Gate D10 is flight NW1538 to RIC (Richmond, Virginia) departing at 17.20, with 51min left before scheduled push-back time from the gate. At D12, flight NW341 to LAX (Los Angeles International) has 41min left before its scheduled 17.10 push-back. Geoffrey P. Jones

Below: As early morning fog from the nearby Mississippi valley clears the end of Minneapolis/St Paul runway 19R, a Northwest Airlines Boeing 757-251 touches down. Geoffrey P. Jones

Above: *Ex-Republic Airlines DC-9-14 N8911E is pictured at Detroit in October 1987 in the immediate post-Republic merger colours. It is still part of the Northwest fleet (Fleet No 9152).* Tony Carre

Below: *Boeing 727s were first delivered to Northwest in November 1964: N285US is a 727-251, built in 1977 and delivered new to Northwest in August 1977. Seen here taxying at Detroit in October 1987.* Tony Carre

Detroit

Detroit's Wayne County Metropolitan Airport (DTW) is ranked as the world's sixth busiest airport in terms of operations (take-offs and landings), is 14th in the world in terms of passenger numbers and is now the US's ninth largest airport by passenger volume. Northwest and KLM have a huge presence here, representing over 80% of the traffic currently using the airport. Currently there are 366 (71%) Northwest jet departures per day from here and 148 (29%) Northwest Airlink flights. These account for over 1,000 aircraft movements per day at DTW.

Biggest growth area in recent years at DTW has been in international passenger traffic, almost wholly due to Northwest Airlines and development of services to Europe and Asia. A total of 3.141 million passengers flew from DTW on international flights in 1997.

There are currently seven domestic concourses at Detroit plus the M. Berry Terminal for international traffic. Northwest Airlines occupies most of the 27 gates of 'C' Concourse, all 19 gates of 'D' Concourse, all 18 gates of 'E' Concourse, nine of the 14 gates of 'F' Concourse and all of the 12 gates of 'G' Concourse. 'G' is occupied wholly by Northwest Airlink operators Mesaba and Express Airlines 1.

In 1997 the DTW Airport Authority and Northwest finalised agreement to construct a new 'mid-field' terminal as part of a $1.6 billion expansion programme, part of which is a $786 million terminal with 74 gates. This will bring the airport's total number of gates to 173. In 1997 DTW handled 31.588 million passengers.

Memphis

Memphis Municipal Airport was officially opened on 15 June 1929, and the following year was being used by the US Air Mail CAM carriers, American Airlines and Chicago & Southern Airways, and handling 15 passengers a day. By 1959, one million passengers had used the airport. In 1969, after major expansion, it was renamed Memphis International Airport, it had 22 gate positions and was served by seven scheduled airlines. In 1985, Republic Airlines chose Memphis as one of its three major hub airports and when Republic was taken over by Northwest Airlines in 1986 it became one of Northwest's major hubs. The first nonstop transatlantic service to Memphis was inaugurated by KLM from Amsterdam on 27 June 1995; a function of the Northwest/KLM alliance. This service continues daily.

Express Airlines 1 had been formed in 1985 in Atlanta, Georgia but soon adopted Memphis as its main operational centre. From 1987 onwards it became a Northwest Airlink operator, flying commuter schedules to 20 destinations from Memphis. There are currently a total of 212 daily Northwest departures from Memphis, 111 (52%) of them mainline jet services and the other 101 (48%) Northwest Airlink. There are three main concourses at Memphis, Northwest currently occupying all 43 gates of 'B' Concourse and 11 gates of 'A' Concourse, the 'A' gates mainly used by Northwest Airlink.

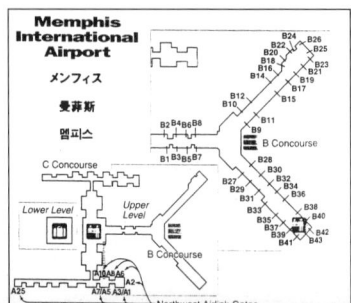

Tokyo Narita

Northwest's Tokyo Narita hub is another of the assets gradually developed since the airline's first pioneering Great Circle schedule from the US to Asia in July 1947. Around 90% of Northwest's Pacific flying touches Japan, Narita, Osaka/Kansai or Nagoya. Northwest is also the largest international, non-Japanese airline operator in Japan, with 10% of all tickets sold internationally being for Northwest flights.

Unlike the US, most airport gates (known at Narita as 'spots'), are not owned by the airline but by the airport authority. The Narita Airport Authority usually honours Northwest's requests for the spot locations, although they do have the final say. The allocation of spots is a day-to-day procedure, mainly on circular Satellite 4 (spots 40 to 48): if all contact gates are occupied, which happens almost daily, a bus or remote gate is used. The total number of spots available at Narita is 91 and during a normal day Northwest uses 15 of them (or 16.5%).

As a measure of Northwest's dominance at Narita, it operates 130 flights per week from here, 13.4% of Narita's 968 total weekly flights. All of Northwest's flights from Narita are operated by Boeing 747 aircraft with the exception of its Guam flight, which is a DC-10.

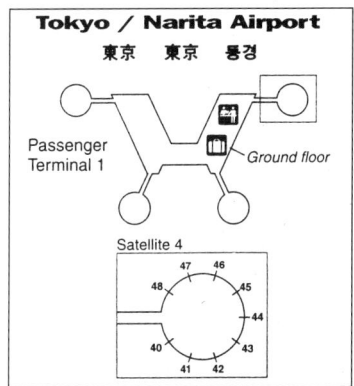

Osaka/Kansai

Osaka/Kansai was opened in September 1994 and immediately Northwest started operations with 18 flights per week. Since then, the number of Northwest flights has increased by 170%. Northwest now operates 49 flights per week from here (7.4% of Osaka/Kansai's 658 total weekly flights). The airport has a total of 37 gates, of which Northwest uses five gates or 13.5% per day.

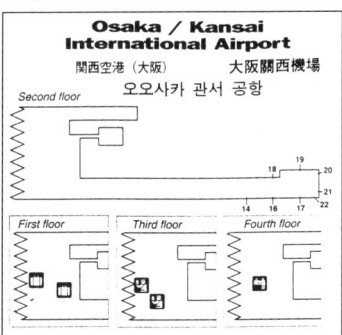

Northwest's Top 10 Markets, 1997 (on passenger numbers)

1. Honolulu-Tokyo (Narita)
2. Chicago (Midway)-Minneapolis/St Paul
3. Detroit-Orlando International
4. Detroit-Chicago (O'Hare)
5. Honolulu-Osaka/Kansai
6. Minneapolis/St Paul-Phoenix
7. Minneapolis/St Paul-San Francisco
8. Los Angeles International-Minneapolis/St Paul
9. Detroit-New York (LaGuardia)
10. Denver-Minneapolis/St Paul

Above: *Taxying at Detroit in June 1997, Boeing 757-251 N511US, Fleet No 5511.* Geoffrey P. Jones

Below: *N150US (c/n 46759) lining up for take-off at Minneapolis/St Paul in June 1995. Delivered new to Northwest Airlines in July 1973, it is one of 22 in the first batch of DC-10-40s delivered between November 1972 and December 1974.* Geoffrey P. Jones

Above: *Northwest Boeing 727-251 N202US (Fleet No 2202 on the nosewheel undercarriage door and on the rear fuselage behind the engine) is carefully tugged to the taxiway at Detroit in June 1997.* Geoffrey P. Jones

Below: *Airbus N335NW A320-211 at the jetway during turnaround at Detroit in June 1997. Northwest, together with alliance partner, KLM, account for around 80% of the passenger traffic at this airport.* Geoffrey P. Jones

Above: All gates at Detroit's 'E' and 'D' Concourses are occupied by Northwest Airlines aircraft in June 1997. A major $786 million programme for a new terminal with an additional 74 gates was agreed by the DTW Airport Authority in 1997. Geoffrey P. Jones

Above: James Tallant, Northwest's Duty Operations Manager at the Detroit control centre in June 1997, has the airline at his fingertips! Every flight and every aircraft on the Northwest network that will impact his Detroit operation is accessible via the computerised displays on the two screens in front of him. Geoffrey P. Jones

Above: Kerbside check-in for the bags of passengers using Northwest's domestic flights is a widespread and popular phenomenon at most of the bigger airports served. This is part of kerbside check-in at Minneapolis/St Paul. D. S. Osborne

Above: Five Express Airlines 1 Saab 340 aircraft, with the tail of a Jetstream 31 and nose of an A320 behind, during a 'bank' (group of connecting flights) at Northwest's third largest domestic hub, Memphis, Tennessee in June 1995. Geoffrey P. Jones

Above: *The upward-hinging nose door of the Boeing 747-251F freighter makes the aircraft ideal for transportation of long items of cargo.*
Northwest Airlines

Below: *A DC-10-40 (N153US) on the left and DC-10-30 (N228NW) on the right, with the Minneapolis skyline as a backdrop in June 1997. The tail-mounted Pratt & Whitney engine gives the aircraft on the left a slightly different profile to the General Electric-powered aircraft on the right.* Geoffrey P. Jones

Above: *In the rich early-morning light in June 1998 at Minneapolis/St Paul, Northwest Airlines Airbus A320-211 N313US. Northwest was the US launch customer for the A320, a major breakthrough for Airbus Industrie.*
Geoffrey P. Jones

Below: *Nosed in to London Gatwick's South Terminal in June 1995, Northwest Boeing 747-251B N614US (Fleet No 6614). 747s are no longer used by Northwest on its transatlantic services to London, DC-10s now being preferred.*
Geoffrey P. Jones

Northwest Cargo

With eight dedicated Boeing 747-200F aircraft, Northwest Cargo would be one of the world's largest cargo airlines in its own right. In 1997 Northwest Cargo was ranked sixth largest airline in the world in terms of freight carriage, representing a total of 681,000 tons: in 1996 it was ranked fourth.

Trans-Pacific flying is where the majority of the 747-200Fs' revenue is earned, and in 1997, with revised schedules, flying time was increased by 10.5%, helping to generate a record revenue of $790 million, a 5.7% increase over 1996's figure. This increased utilisation represents the addition of a fleet average of 30hr per week flying time, rising during peak months to a 60hr increase. Revenue earned from the cargo operation represents over 7% of the airline's total revenue.

The Boeing 747-200F has a cargo capacity of approximately 235,215lb/105 tons. The aircraft have nose-doors that can handle 10ft M-1 or 20ft M-2 cargo containers as well as the more conventional under-belly LD-7 containers. As well as the dedicated cargo aircraft, Northwest in common with most other major airlines carries significant quantities of cargo and mail in passenger aircraft belly holds, usually containerised and on both international and domestic services.

When Northwest took delivery of the first of an order for three 747-200Fs in 1975, scepticism was the reaction of the other major US airlines. Northwest became the first and only US passenger airline to buy these specialist freighter aircraft from Boeing. As well as the front cargo door, the Northwest aircraft were also fitted with side-load doors to facilitate the loading of vehicles. Under the direction of long-serving President Donald Nyrop, a senior team of Northwest analysts set out to completely re-evaluate the air-freight market, particularly on its important routes between the US and the Orient. Northwest Cargo, with its 747-200Fs, pioneered the large-scale transport of commodities such as asparagus, citrus fruit, lettuce, cherries and salmon. Oil companies also found the nose door and the 190ft-long hold particularly useful for transporting lengthy specialist pipes and equipment from the US to the developing oilfields in southeast Asia.

Northwest's cargo business grew so rapidly that after a year a fourth aircraft was ordered, and in due course the fleet increased in size to its current eight aircraft. Northwest had also pioneered the use of a computerised cargo analysis service for customers, so that they could make an almost instant comparison of costs between sea and air transportation. Northwest also 'hit the spot' with the burgeoning Asian electronics, optical and audio-visual goods manufacturing industries. These relatively lightweight, high-value goods started to flood in to the US, many of them transported by Northwest Cargo.

In 1972, Northwest's cargo sales, including mail, totalled $32.4 million. By 1985, after 10 years of 747-200F operations, this figure had increased dramatically to $408.5 million and to $790 million by 1997. The importance of cargo to Northwest is well illustrated in this 1997 figure, which represented nearly 8% of the airline group's total revenue.

It was a cargo service that pioneered Northwest's presence in Europe in 1979. The 747-200F freight flight originated in Boston and New York and served Glasgow and Copenhagen. The airline's first passenger service to Europe followed soon after.

Northwest Cargo opened its new 'cross-loading' hub at Anchorage, Alaska in 1997 as part of its continuing development of trans-Pacific air freight. There is now sufficient room for five 747 freighters to be cross-loaded there simultaneously — not always Northwest aircraft.

This system sees two freighters arrive in Anchorage from Asia at approximately the same time. One is bound for Los Angeles and the other for Chicago. Each, however,

Above: *Northwest broke with tradition among passenger airlines in 1975 when it took delivery of its first Boeing 747-251F, a dedicated 100% freighter aircraft. Northwest Cargo now operates a fleet of eight 747-200Fs and is one of the world's largest freight airlines. N640US is seen here at Minneapolis/St Paul in June 1995.* Geoffrey P. Jones

has freight destined for the other's destination. The aircraft are parked next to each other and Northwest Cargo's Anchorage team transfer the Chicago-bound freight from the Los Angeles-bound aircraft and vice versa. It is not a new concept, and operates on a much larger basis at the Federal Express small-packet hub at Memphis.

Because of the importance to Northwest Cargo of its trans-Pacific links, it operates a major air freight hub at Tokyo (Narita), including another cross-loading facility. From mid-1997, as part of the airline's plan to increase aircraft utilisation, less profitable US domestic stopovers for the freighter fleet were axed and long-haul schedules enhanced, reducing the number of take-offs and landings and increasing the time in the air. A new midweek freighter service from Tokyo to New York was added, along with two additional flights per week from Tokyo, one to San Francisco and the other to Los Angeles. Similar services from Osaka to the US were increased from two flights to four flights a week. From 1 February 1998 a new twice-weekly Northwest Cargo service from the US to Manila in the Philippines was inaugurated, adding 220 tons of trans-Pacific capacity to the market. The service departs from Chicago on Sundays and from New York on Wednesdays, with intermediate stops in Anchorage, Tokyo and Bangkok. Manila has become Northwest Cargo's seventh market in Asia served by all-freight 747-200Fs, the others being Tokyo, Osaka, Hong Kong, Taipei, Bangkok and Singapore.

Above: *Simmons Airlines ATR-42 N425MQ, a Northwest Airlink operator's aircraft in the 1980s at Detroit.* Tony Carre

Below: *Ex-North Central Airlines Convair 440-82, converted to a Convair 580 as N7743U and one of 14 of the type in the Republic Airlines fleet at the time of its takeover by Northwest in 1986. It is seen here in Northwest colours at Detroit in October 1987.* Tony Carre

Above: *Artwork painted in 1997 on Northwest's 'World Plane', Boeing 747 N670US, to celebrate the 50th anniversary of the airline's first scheduled trans-Pacific flight.* Northwest Airlines

Below: *Just after delivery from British Aerospace in June 1997, the first Mesaba Airlines RJ85, N501XJ, is affectionately named 'Sparky' by pilots and engineering staff of the airline.* Geoffrey P. Jones

The US/Japan aviation agreement signed at the beginning of 1998 has considerably helped Northwest Cargo as well as Northwest Airlines passenger services. As a result, Northwest's 'Fifth Freedom Rights' to carry passengers and cargo traffic between any city in Japan and any city in the Asia/Pacific region were enhanced. On 6 April 1998, Northwest extended its Seattle-Osaka service to Taipei, Taiwan, and it became a daily service, complementing the daily departures from Osaka to Detroit, Minneapolis/St Paul, Los Angeles and Honolulu. While these new trans-Pacific schedules are important for the passenger, they further enhance the airline's cargo flexibility and capacity for belly-hold, containerised freight, often more lucrative than the passengers above.

All these developments confirm Northwest Cargo as the largest cargo

Above: *Ex Swissair HB-IHE, Northwest Airlines Douglas DC-10-30 N221NW approaching the gate at Minneapolis/St. Paul in June 1995.* Geoffrey P. Jones

carrier among US combination (passenger and cargo service) airlines — and still the only US combination carrier to operate Boeing 747-200F freighters.

Below: *Loose mail bags and containerised freight being unloaded from the rear belly hold of Boeing 747-251B N614US on a damp Minneapolis/St Paul ramp in June 1995.* Geoffrey P. Jones

Above: *An ex-Eastern Air Lines and then Southern Airways aircraft, built in 1966, DC-9-14 N8903E has now been retired from the Northwest fleet. It is seen in Northwest's 'new' livery at Minneapolis/St Paul in 1995, passing DC-9-31 N915RW in the 1970s/80s Northwest colours.* Geoffrey P. Jones

Above: *Being serviced during turnaround at Minneapolis/St Paul in June 1995, Boeing 727-251 N296US is one of 40 727s still in the Northwest fleet in 1998.* Geoffrey P. Jones

Above: *N768NC Douglas DC-9-51, seen taxying at Detroit in 1995, was a North Central Airlines aircraft until the July 1979 merger with Southern Airways to form Republic.* Geoffrey P. Jones

Below: *Nosing its way to the jetway on 'B' Concourse at Memphis in June 1995, Northwest DC-9-32 N987US, Fleet No 9987, was manufactured in December 1971 and is ex-Austrian Airlines OE-LDF, one of six DC-9-32s in the fleet fitted with long-range fuel tanks.* Geoffrey P. Jones

Above: *Mesaba Airlines operates 17 DHC-8-102As as part of its Northwest Airlink operation at Minneapolis/St Paul. They are currently being phased out of service.* Geoffrey P. Jones

Above: *Since 1993, the Northwest/KLM alliance has been the envy of the air transport industry. All aircraft of these two mainline carriers display this logo, plus some aircraft of associate airlines.* Geoffrey P. Jones

Training

A wholly owned and indirect subsidiary of the Northwest Airlines Corporation, Northwest Aerospace Training Corporation (NATCO) is located at Eagan, Minneapolis/St Paul and is an acknowledged leader in air travel safety training for pilots, flight crews, ground services and systems operations control personnel. NATCO was the first large jet training facility to become certificated under the Federal Air Regulation (FAR) Part 142. This enables NATCO to provide airlines and jet operators with a complete package of pilot training services as required by the US Federal Aviation Administration (FAA).

NATCO was originally created as a result of the 1986 Northwest/Republic merger to provide pilot training to the much enlarged airline, and to other airlines from around the world. It is now the largest independent airline-affiliated training centre in the world.

The primary feature of NATCO is its 26 flight simulators. These cover all aircraft types currently in the Northwest fleet, plus one Saab 340B simulator used by Northwest Airlink airline, Mesaba. Two other Northwest flight simulators are located at Long Beach, California and one at Vancouver, Canada. NATCO has a floor area of 270,000 square feet and could be expanded to house a further six simulators. To support the simulator training there are 10 classrooms, 78 briefing rooms and an emergency room.

When pilots are hired by an airline, they receive 10-12 days of ground school training at NATCO and then go on to receive approximately 10 days (or 40 hours) of simulator training on the type of aircraft to which they have been assigned. They are able to be completely certificated by the FAA in the simulator before they fly the jump seat (the non-command seat between the Captain and the First Officer on the aircraft flightdeck) for a period of approximately 25hr of flight time, before being placed for the first time in the First Officer's seat (the right-hand seat) on scheduled flights.

Below: *The three throttle levers in the centre console show that this is the flightdeck of a DC-10, in fact DC-10-30 N223NW. The three-man crew (still including a Flight Engineer) prepares for push-back at London Gatwick for Northwest's daily flight to Detroit.* Geoffrey P. Jones

Above: *Almost exactly a year after the delivery of Northwest's first Airbus A320, N307US (Fleet No 3207) is seen taxying for take-off at San Francisco International Airport in June 1990.* Geoffrey P. Jones

NATCO has created two specific computer-based training programmes for the Boeing 747-400 and the Airbus A320 aircraft. The advantages of these, like other similar training packages, are:

- the prohibitively expensive cost of training on real aircraft, linked to the out-of-service time that would be necessary;
- situations and manoeuvres that may be unsafe in a real aircraft can be safely simulated to train a pilot to react to their possible onset;
- pilots can keep pace with the rapid advances in aviation technology.

In 1997 NATCO provided training for 106 airlines, operators and government agencies worldwide. Particularly strong are NATCO's links with Asia: 14 major Asian airlines currently have contracts for training with NATCO. The corporation is also training dispatchers for China's Civil Aviation Administration.

Northwest's affiliation with KLM means that many KLM staff, including pilots and flight attendants, are trained at NATCO, another of the many largely-unseen benefits of the Northwest/KLM link-up. In January 1998, NATCO and KLM exercised their joint purchasing power to buy two new simulators, one a new Airbus A320 simulator and the other for the Boeing 737-800. Both will be supplied by Canadian firm CAE, the A320 simulator scheduled for November 1998 delivery to Eagan, and the 737-800 simulator to Schipol East in Amsterdam.

NATCO signed a major contract with Atlas Air Freight in January 1998 and one of its 747-200F simulators is now located within the Northwest complex, enabling Atlas pilots to undergo training as well as those who fly Northwest's own fleet of eight

747-200Fs. NATCO will also train all Atlas 747-200 and 747-400 crews.

During 1997, more than 3,100 Northwest line and hangar mechanics began a training regime at NATCO in human-factor appreciation. This training emphasises teamwork, open communications, workplace discipline and situational awareness to reduce human error. This is now made mandatory by the FAA and Northwest implemented such training prior to the FAA's mandate.

Northwest Airlines Simulators

Located at Eagan, Minneapolis/St Paul

Type	Supplier	Computer	Visual Display	Motion Axes	Entered Service
A320-200	T-CSF	Encore 32/97	SPX500/150	6	1990
A320-200	Link/NATCO	Encore 32/67	SPX200CT/150	6	1990
A320-200	Link/NATCO	Encore 32/67	SPX250CT	6	1997
A320-200	CAE	IBM 6000	ESIG3350/180	6	1998
B727-200	Link	PDP 11/45	Vital IV	6	1994
B727-200	Link	Encore 32/7780	SP3T	6	1984
B727-200	Link	Encore 32/77	SP1	6	1983
B747-200	CAE	TI980BB	Vital IV	6	1976
B747-200	Link	Encore 32/77	SP1	6	1982
B747-200F	Link-Miles	Encore 32/77	DNVS	6	1997 (Atlas)
B747-200	Link/NATCO	Encore 32/67	SPX200CT/150	6	1990
B747-400	CAE	Encore MultiSEL	SPX500/150	6	1989
B747-400	Link/NATCO	Encore 32/67	SPX200CT/150	6	1990
B757-200	Link	Encore 32/77	SP3T	6	1985
B757-200	CAE	Encore MultiSEL	SPX500/150	6	1990
B757-200	Link-Miles	Encore 32/67	SPX200CT	6	1990
DC-10-30	Link-Miles	Xioix X-7/GP4	SP1T	6	
DC-10-40	Link	GP-4/Encore 32/27	SP1	6	1973
DC-9-10	Link	GP-4	N2500	3	1966
DC-9-30	Link	PDP 11/45	Vital IV	6	1975
DC-9-30	AE	TI980A/B	Vital IV	6	1975
DC-9-30	Link/NATCO	Encore MultiSEL	SPX500	6	1990
DC-9-30	Link/NATCO	EncoreMultiSEL	SPX500/150	6	1990
DC-9-30 (ex-MD-80)	NATCO/CAE	VAX 11/780	Vital IV	6	
MD-80	CAE	VAX 11/780	Vital IV/4w	6	1983
Saab 340B	CAE	IBM 6000	n/a	n/a	n/a

at Long Beach, California

Type	Supplier	Computer	Visual Display	Motion Axes	Entered Service
MD-82	Rediffusion	Encore 32/67	SPX200CT	6	1993
MD-82/87	Rediffusion	MultiSEL	SPX200T/150	6	1990

at Vancouver, Canada

Type	Supplier	Computer	Visual Display	Motion Axes	Entered Service
B747-400	Link/NATCO	Encore 32/67	SPX200CT/150	6	1990

Above: *The Northwest/KLM alliance followed the granting of anti-trust immunity by the US Department of Transportation in January 1993.* Geoffrey P. Jones

Aircraft

Northwest's aircraft fleet at June 1998 numbered 408 aircraft (excluding Northwest Airlink aircraft), with a further 112 on order. As a comparison of the growth of the airline's fleet, it numbered only 119 aircraft in 1984 and 139 in 1986. Fleet growth has occurred to take account of the considerable increase in the number of passengers carried per annum, rising from 35.8 million in 1988 to 54.7 million in 1997, but not proportionally, as load factors have also increased over this 10-year period. Northwest's average fleet age at January 1998 was 21 years.

Northwest Airlines currently has the biggest fleet of Douglas DC-9s in the world. These are the older models, the DC-9-10 (78 seats), the DC-9-30 (100 seats), the DC-9-40 (112 seats) and the DC-9-50 (119/122 seats). Northwest currently has 181 of these aircraft in its operational fleet and has recently purchased further DC-9-30s, although some of the older, short-bodied DC-9-10/15s are currently being phased out of service. The DC-9-15s, some of them ex-Republic Airlines aircraft that were new in 1967, are being replaced on the thinner mainline Northwest route system by RJ85s of Northwest Jet Airlink partner Mesaba Airlines. Three second-hand DC-9-30s were acquired by Northwest in 1997: in 1996 it purchased seven, and in 1995, 14.

The DC-9 fleet has been the subject of considerable investment in recent years, on engine hush-kitting, systems upgrades and internal cabin refurbishment — by 1998 over 75% of the DC-9 fleet will be hush-kitted.

Northwest's other Douglas-derived twinjet is the McDonnell Douglas MD-82, of which eight are currently in the fleet. These are also a legacy of the October 1986 acquisition of Republic Airlines which flew an all-Douglas DC-9/McDonnell Douglas MD-80 fleet until just before its takeover.

Below: *DC-9-51 N782NC at Miami in March 1986 is in the revised colours of Republic Airlines, adopted in the mid-1980s just prior to the takeover by Northwest. This aircraft is still in the Northwest fleet, with Fleet No 9873.*
Geoffrey P. Jones

Northwest's MD-82s seat 148 passengers, 12 first-class and 136 coach.

The first of Northwest's order for 22 (although only 21 were taken up) Douglas DC-10-40s began arriving at Minneapolis/St Paul in November 1972. These were customised for Northwest's oriental services, using Pratt & Whitney JT9D engines, as fitted to the Boeing 747s already in their fleet, rather than the General Electric engines Douglas previously fitted to all DC-10s. The new engines increased the range of the DC-10-40 by 1,205 miles. To demonstrate their range, Northwest flew a special nonstop Los Angeles to Hong Kong flight (7,677 miles) in 1972 in a time of 14hr 44min. Twenty-one DC-10-40s remain in the Northwest fleet and DC-10-30s were first acquired secondhand from Swissair in 1991. The airline's affair with the Douglas trijet has continuied into 1998, making a total of 36 DC-10s in service, with three additional low-houred DC-10-30ERs (built in 1982) being acquired from Thai Airways International, and further aircraft of the type being located for possible purchase for long-haul work and higher-density, long-range US routes. The DC-10-40s have seating for either 281 or 290 passengers, depending on exact model, with 34 seats in World Business Class. The DC-10-30s (15 in the fleet) also have seating for 281, with 34 in World Business Class.

Boeing 747s have been an integral part of most international airlines' fleets since the type's first service entry with PanAm in January 1970. The first of 10 Boeing 747-100s ordered by Northwest followed soon after, the first service with the type being flown on 22 June 1970 between Minneapolis/St Paul and New York. Subsequently Boeing 747-200s were ordered, followed by dedicated freighter 747-200Fs and then in December 1985 an order for 10 Boeing 747-400s. The current Northwest fleet still contains Boeing 747s of these four types, although the three older 747-100s will soon be phased out of service. Twenty-two Boeing 747-200s are still in service, with a major internal refurbishment programme planned for them over the next two years and with seating for 367 or 376 passengers. The eight dedicated Boeing 747-200Fs continue in service as a vital element of Northwest's cargo capability. Northwest (at the time Northwest Orient Airlines) was the launch customer for the Boeing 747-400 in October 1985, with an order for 10 aircraft. These 747-400s are powered by PW4000 series engines, configured in a three-class layout (First/World Business/Coach), and seat 418 passengers. First delivery of Northwest's first Boeing 747-400s was on 26 January 1989 on route-proving flights, with service entry five days later on domestic routes between Minneapolis and Phoenix. Direct New York-Tokyo services with the 747-400 commenced in June 1989.

Boeing 727s have been the backbone of most US airline fleets since the first of the type flew in 1963. In its time — between 1964 and 1984 — it was the best selling jetliner in the world, with 1,831 sold. A short- and medium-range airliner, Northwest's first Boeing 727 entered service in 1964. Eventually a total of 65 were in the fleet, nine of them the original model 727-100, but 56 of them the 727-200. Due to attrition, age, etc, the Northwest Boeing 727 fleet has now reduced, confined to 727-200s, of which 40 are current, configured in a two-class layout (First/Coach) and seating 149 passengers.

Twenty Boeing 757-251s were ordered by Northwest, the first entering service on 15 March 1985 between Minneapolis/St Paul and Washington DC's National airport. A first follow-on order for 10 more followed, and the fleet size now numbers 48 aircraft. The 757 was considered the ultimate development of the Boeing 727, although it bore no external resemblance to the type. The fuselage cross-sectional area was the same, as was the three-seat/aisle/three-seat cabin plan. The Boeing 757 first flew in February 1982, had a completely new flightdeck with an integrated digital system for flight control and a glass cockpit for two-crew operation. Northwest's Boeing 757s were fitted with two underwing Pratt & Whitney PW2037 turbofans, which, linked to the newly designed super-critical wing, gave a take-off run about 1,250ft less than the equivalently-loaded Boeing 727. It also burned 42% less fuel than the 727 and was much quieter, both inside and out. A further 25 Boeing 757-251s are on order and will gradually replace Boeing 727s, the seating arrangement configured in a two-class layout (First/Coach) for either 190 or 194 passengers.

Northwest's order for Airbus Industrie A320-200s in 1986 was a ground-breaking achievement by this European company, and Northwest became the first US carrier to take delivery of the type on 8 June 1989. With CFM56 turbofan engines and revolutionary fly-by-wire side-stick controls, Northwest currently has 53 of the A320 in its fleet, the first 50 aircraft now being supplemented by deliveries from the follow-up order for a further 20, delivery of which commenced in January 1998. Seating arrangement in the A320 is configured in a two-class layout (First/Coach) for 150 passengers. Northwest also signed an agreement of purchase with Airbus Industrie valued at $6 billion in 1997, covering the purchase of 50 of the A319 aircraft for delivery at the rate of 10 per year commencing in 1999. The order also had options for up to 100 additional Airbus family aircraft, although in May 1998 Boeing entered the fray with a campaign to sell Northwest up to 100 of the new Boeing 717 (the former MD-95) as part of Northwest's DC-9 replacement programme. These aircraft are intended primarily to serve domestic growth needs from Northwest's three strategic mainland US hubs.

Sixteen Airbus A330s are also on order, but a delivery schedule is currently uncertain.

Operating Aircraft in Northwest's Fleet (Correct to June 1998)

Type	Number in Fleet	Seating Total	Seating Arrangement
B747-400	10	418	F/18, WBC/62, MC/338
B747-200	22	369/370	F/8-12, WBC/63-66, MC/296
B747-100	3	450	WBC/34, MC/416
B747-200F	8	-	
DC-10-40	21	281/290	WBC/34, MC/247-256
DC-10-30	15	281	WBC/34, MC/247
B757-251	48	190/194	F/14, MC/176-180
B727-200	40	149	F/12, MC/137
A320-200	53	150	F/12, MC/138
MD-82	8	148	F/12, MC/136
DC-9-50	35	119/122	F/12-16, MC/107-110
DC-9-40	12	112	F/12-16, MC/94-100
DC-9-30	114	100	F/16, MC/84
DC-9-10	19	78	F/8-14, MC/64-70

Fleet Total 408
F=first, WBC=world business class, MC=coach

Firm Orders

B747-400	4
B757-251	25
A319	50
A320-200	17
A330	16
Total	112

Aircraft Specifications

Boeing 747-400

Prototype first flight	29 April 1988
Wingspan	211ft (64.31m)
Wing area	5,600sq ft (520.25sq m)
Length	231ft 10in (70.66m)
Height	63ft 8in (19.41m)
Max seating	2 flightdeck crew, 418 passengers
Cargo volume	6,025cu ft (170.6cu m)
Fuel capacity	45,012 imp gal (204,355 litres)
Empty weight	402,400lb (182,526kg)
Maximum take-off weight	800,000lb (362,880kg)
Range	6,055nm (6,972 miles) at Max TOW
	7,270nm (8,371 miles) at reduced weight
Cruising speed	Mach 0.85
Powerplant	Four x Pratt & Whitney PW4056
	57,100lb thrust each (254kN)
Service ceiling	42,000ft (12,810m)
First delivery to NW	26 January 1989

Above: *The first Boeing 747-400 to be delivered to Northwest in January 1989, N661US (ex N401PW). Northwest was the launch customer for the larger and long-range 747-400 when it placed an order for 10 in October 1985. All are still in the fleet.* Howard Cloc

Boeing 747-200, 747-100, 747-200F

	747-200	747-100	747-200F
Prototype first flight	11 October 1970	9 February 1969	30 November 1971
Wingspan	195ft 8in (59.64m)	195ft 8in (59.64m)	195ft 8in (59.64m)
Wing area	5,500sq ft (511sq m)	5,500sq ft (511sq m)	5,500sq ft (511sq m)
Length	231ft 10in (70.66m)	231ft 10in (70.66m)	231ft 10in (70.66m)
Height	63ft 5in (19.33m)	63ft 5in (19.33m)	63ft 5in (19.33m)
Max seating	3 flightdeck	3 flightdeck	3 flightdeck
	369/370 passengers	454 passengers	none
Cargo volume	6,190cu ft (175.4cu m)	24,260cu ft (687cu m)	n/a
Fuel capacity	44,952 imp gal	40,339 imp gal	44,952 imp gal
Empty weight	374,700lb	373,500lb	342,200lb
	(169,961kg)	(169,417kg)	(155,219kg)
Max take-off weight	785,000lb	710,000lb	800,000lb
	(356,070kg)	(322,050kg)	(362,875kg)
Range	6,550nm	5,500nm	7,900nm
	(7,542 miles)	(6,333 miles)	(9,091 miles)
Cruising speed	527kt (607mph)	525kt (604mph)	527kt (607mph)
Powerplant (x4)	P&W JT9D-7F	P&W JT7A	P&W JT9D-7F
	46,950lb thrust	43,500lb thrust	48,000lb thrust
Service ceiling	39,000ft (11,890m)	39,000ft (11,890m)	39,000ft (11,890m)
First delivery to NW	March 1971	April 1970	July 1975

Right: *Boeing 747-251B N628US in the old Northwest Orient markings at Detroit in October 1987. There are currently 22 Boeing 747-200 series aircraft in the Northwest fleet.* Tony Carre

McDonnell Douglas DC-10-30 and DC-10-40

	DC-10-30	DC-10-40
First flight	29 August 1970 (DC-10-10)	
Wingspan	165ft 4in (50.39m)	165ft 4in (50.39m)
Wing area	3,647sq ft (338.8sq m)	3,647sq ft (338.8sq m)
Length	180ft 8in (55.06m)	180ft 8in (55.06m)
Height	58ft 1in (17.7m)	58ft 1in (17.7m)
Seating	3 flightdeck	3 flightdeck
	281 passengers	281/290 passengers
Cargo volume	3,655cu ft (103.5cu m)	3,655cu ft (103.5cu m)

Fuel capacity	245,566lb (111,420kg)	245,566lb (111,420kg)
Weight empty	267,197lb (121,198kg)	271,062lb (122,951kg)
Max take-off weight	580,000lb (263,085kg)	572,000lb (259,450kg)
Max range with max fuel	4,000nm (4,606 miles)	4,050nm (4,663 miles)
Cruising speed	490kt (564mph)	498kt (573mph)
Powerplant (x3)	GE CF6-50C	P&W JT-9D-20
	51,000lb (227kN) thrust	49,400lb (220kN) thrust
Service ceiling	33,400ft (10,180m)	32,700ft (9,965m)
First delivery to NW	Secondhand from 1991	November 1972

Above: *This Douglas DC-10-40 was in 1973 one of the first DC-10s delivered to Northwest Airlines (the very first was in November 1972). N141US is pictured here in the 'old' colours at New York's John F. Kennedy International Airport in October 1987.* Tony Carre

Boeing 757-251

First flight	19 February 1982
Wingspan	124ft 10in (38.05m)
Wing area	1,994sq ft (185.25sq m)
Length	155ft 3in (47.32m)
Height	44ft 6in (13.56m)
Seating	2 flightdeck
	190/194 passengers
Cargo volume	1,790cu ft (50.7cu m)
Fuel capacity	75,500lb (34,277kg)
Max take-off weight	220,000lb (100,000kg)
Range	2,493nm (2,867 miles)
Cruising speed	522kt (600mph)
Powerplant (x2)	P & W PW2037 turbofan
	38,200lb thrust each
Service ceiling	48,000ft (14,630m)
First delivered to NW	February 1985

Above: *Boeing 757-251 N504US, Fleet No 5504, City of Los Angeles, seen in Northwest's 'old' colours, taxying at Detroit in October 1987. The first 33 of Northwest's 757s are named after various US cities.* Tony Carre

Above: *Climbing out over the Potomac River from Washington National Airport in June 1990 is Northwest Airlines Boeing 727-251 N278US, since retired from the fleet.* Geoffrey P. Jones

Boeing 727-200

First flight	9 February 1963 (B727-100)
	27 July 1967 (B727-200)
Wingspan	108ft (32.92m)
Wing area	1,700sq ft (157.9sq m)
Length	153ft 2in (46.72m)
Height	34ft (10.37m)
Seating	3 flightdeck
	149 passengers
Cargo volume	1,454cu ft (41.18cu m)
Empty weight	101,100lb (45,900kg)
Max take-off weight	178,000lb (80,812kg)
Range with max fuel	2,400nm (2,760 miles)
Range with max payload	2,140nm (2,461 miles)
Powerplant (x3)	P & W JT8D-15A or -17 turbofan
	14,000lb thrust each
Maximum ceiling	35,000ft (10,670m)
First delivered to NW	November 1964 (B727-100)

Airbus Industrie A320-211

First flight	22 February 1987
Wingspan	111ft 3in (33.91m)
Wing area	1,317.5sq ft (122.4sq m)
Length	123ft 3in (37.57m)
Height	38ft 8.5in (11.8m)
Seating	2 flightdeck
	150 passengers
Cargo volume	1,369cu ft (39.08cu m)
Fuel capacity	5,248 imp gal (23,859 litres)
	42,238lb (19,159kg)
Empty weight	87,634lb (39,750kg)
Maximum take-off weight	162,040lb (73,500kg)
Range with max fuel	2,930nm (3,374 miles)
Cruising speed	Mach 0.78 to 0.8
Powerplant (x2)	CFM International CFM-56-5A1
	25,000lb (111.21kN) thrust each
Maximum ceiling	39,000ft (11,890m)
First delivery to NW	8 June 1989

Right; *In March 1997, the GHI-CA Corporation, a NWA Inc subsidiary, acquired the Minneapolis/St Paul-based Champion Air, a five-aircraft Boeing 727 charter airline. MLT Vacations, another NWA Inc subsidiary, will use Champion for vacation charter flying.*
Geoffrey P. Jones

McDonnell Douglas MD-82

First flight	18 October 1979 (first DC-9 Super 80/MD-80 series)
	8 January 1981 (MD-82)
Wingspan	107ft 10in (32.87m)
Wing area	1,270sq ft (118sq m)
Length	147ft 10in (45.06m)
Height	29ft 8in (9.04m)
Seating	2 flightdeck
	148 passengers
Cargo volume	1,253cu ft (35.48cu m)
Fuel capacity	39,128lb (17,748kg)
	4,812 imp gal (21,876 litres)
Empty weight	78,549lb (35,629kg)
Maximum take-off weight	149,500lb (67,812kg)
Range with max fuel	2,049nm (2,360 miles)
Cruising speed	Mach 0.76/510kt (586mph)
Powerplant (x2)	Pratt & Whitney JT8D-217
	20,000lb (89kN) thrust each
Maximum ceiling	37,000ft (11,285m)
First delivered to NW	October 1986*

* on takeover of Republic Airlines — delivered new to Republic, August 1981-August 1983

Douglas DC-9-10/15, DC-9-30, DC-9-40 and DC-9-50

	DC-9-10/15	DC-9-30	DC-9-40	DC-9-50
First flight	25 Feb 1965	1 Aug 1966	28 Nov 1967	17 Dec 1974
Wingspan	89ft 5in (27.25m)	93ft 5in (28.5m)	93ft 5in (28.5m)	93ft 5in (28.5m)
Length	104ft 5in (31.82m)	119ft 5in (36.43m)	125ft 7in (38.27m)	133ft 7in (40.72m)
Height	29ft 8in (9.04m)	29ft 8in (9.04m)	29ft 8in (9.04m)	29ft 8in (9.04m)
Seating	2 x flightdeck 78 passengers	2 x flightdeck 100 passengers	2 x flightdeck 112 passengers	2 x flightdeck 119/122 passengers
Cargo volume	600cu ft (17cu m)	888cu ft (25.2cu m)	920cu ft (26.03cu m)	966cu ft (27.33cu m)
Max gross TOW	90,700lb (41,141kg)	108,000lb (48,988kg)	114,000lb (57,710kg)	121,000lb (54,885kg)
Powerplant (x2)	P&W JT8D-7B	P&W JT8D-9	P&W JT8D-11	P&W JT8D-17
Thrust (per engine)	14,000lb (6,350kg)	14,500lb (6,577kg)	15,000lb (6,804kg)	16,000lb (7,257kg)
First delivered to NW	Oct 1986 Ex-Republic	Oct 1986 Ex-Republic	Starting 1991 Ex-SAS	Oct 1986 Ex-Republic

Above: One of the oldest DC-9's currently flying in the Northwest fleet, N91S a DC-9-15, Fleet No 9101 was originally delivered to Southern Airways in May 1967, moved to Bonanza Airlines, back to Southern and then to Republic in July 1979. These smaller and older DC-9's are being replaced by Northwest Jet Airlink services with RJ85's. This aircraft was photographed at Witchita, Kansas in June 1995. Geoffrey P. Jones

Above: Douglas DC-9-31 N917RW (ex-N8936E of Eastern Air Lines) landing at Minneapolis/St Paul in 1995. Northwest aircraft carry their fleet or ship number on the nose and tail, this aircraft being No 9958. Geoffrey P. Jones

Northwest Airlink Aircraft Specification

Avro RJ85 (BAe146) (Mesaba Airlines)

First flight	1992
Wingspan	86ft 5in (26.34m)
Length	93ft 8in (28.55m)
Height	28ft 3in (8.61m)
Empty weight	54,000lb (24,494kg)
Max take-off weight	93,000lb (42,184kg)
Seating	2 x flightdeck
	69 passengers
Range	1,450nm (1,670 miles)
Cruise speed	364-432kt (419-497mph)
Powerplant (x4)	Allied Signal LF507-1F turbofans
First delivered to NW/Mesaba	April 1997

Saab 340A and 340B (Mesaba Airlines/Express Airlines 1)

	Saab 340A	Saab 340B
First flight	25 January 1983 (Saab-Fairchild 340 variant)	
Wingspan	70ft 4in (21.44m)	70ft 4in (21.44m)
Length	64ft 9in (19.73m)	64ft 9in (19.73m)
Height	22ft 6in (6.86m)	22ft 11in (6.97m)
Empty weight	17,415lb (7,899kg)	17,945lb (8,140kg)
Max take-off weight	27,275lb (12,372kg)	29,211lb (13,250kg)
Seating	2 x flightdeck	2 x flightdeck
	35 passengers	35 passengers
Range	500nm (576 miles)	805-935nm (927-1,076 m)
Cruise speed	250kt (288mph)	285kt (328mph)
Powerplant (x2)	GE CT7-5A2 turboprop 1,735shp (1,294kW)	GE CT7-9B turboprop 1,750shp (1,305kW)

De Havilland Canada DHC-8-100 (Mesaba Airlines)

First flight	20 June 1983
Wingspan	85ft (25.91m)
Length	73ft (22.25m)
Height	24ft 7in (7.49m)
Empty weight	21,590lb (9,793kg)
Max take-off weight	33,000lb (14,968kg)
Seating	2 x flightdeck
	36 passengers
Range	890nm (1,025 miles)
Cruise speed	268kt (309mph)
Powerplant (x2)	P&W Canada PW120A turboprop 1,800shp (1,432kW)

NB: currently being phased out from the Mesaba fleet.

BAe Jetstream 31 (Express Airlines 1)

First flight	28 March 1980 (converted Handley Page Jetstream)
	18 March 1982 (first production Jetstream 31)
Wingspan	52ft (15.85m)
Length	47ft 1.5in (14.37m)
Height	17ft 5.5in (5.32m)
Empty weight	9,613lb (4,360kg)
Max take-off weight	15,212lb (6,900kg)
Seating	2 x flightdeck
	18 passengers
Range	643nm (740 miles)
Cruise speed	230kt (264mph)
Powerplant (x2)	Garrett TPE331-10UG turboprop
	940shp (701kW) each

Fairchild-Swearingen SA227AC Metro III (Mesaba Airlines)
(type phased out by 1998)

First flight	1966 (original version, the Metro)
	31 December 1981 (Metro IIIA)
Wingspan	57ft (17.37m)
Length	59ft 4in (18.09m)
Height	16ft 8in (5.08m)
Empty weight	8,737lb (3,963kg)
Max take-off weight	14,500lb (6,577kg)
Seating	2 x flightdeck
	19-20 passengers
Range	869nm (1,001 miles)
Cruise speed	278kt (320mph)
Powerplant (x2)	Garrett TPE331-11U-611G turboprop
	1,100shp (820kW) 'wet'

Right: *Passengers disembarking via the integral air-stair of this Northwest Airlink Saab 340A at Minneapolis/St Paul. Northwest Airlink accounts for 153 flights a day from MSP in mid-1998.*
Geoffrey P. Jones

Engineering

Northwest Airlines aircraft are maintained to the highest standards and strictly in accordance with all Federal Aviation Authority (FAA) regulations. The airline's safety record mirrors this with no fatal accidents to Northwest mainline aircraft attributable to maintenance shortfalls for many decades.

About 5,500 mechanics are employed by Northwest, over 10% of the airline's total workforce. Apart from line maintenance staff and engine maintenance, the airline has three main centres for all of its aircraft work:

Minneapolis/St Paul	2,359
Atlanta, Georgia	985
Duluth, Minnesota	279

At Minneapolis/St Paul (MSP), heavy maintenance is undertaken on all of Northwest's Boeing 747, DC-10 and Boeing 757 fleet, together with a portion of the DC-9 work. In addition, as the airline's main base, it also has a huge component shop for the majority of the fleet as well as retaining a huge spares holding. Line support for the 339 daily Northwest Airlines departures from MSP (excluding Airlink) is also centred here along with the airline's engine shops. Staff from Boeing, McDonnell Douglas and Pratt & Whitney as well as the FAA are on permanent secondment at MSP to liaise with Northwest Airlines to ensure the highest standards are maintained.

All heavy maintenance on Northwest's DC-9 fleet is carried out at Atlanta, a location seeming somewhat out of place with the airline's route structure. The explanation is historical — Atlanta was one of Southern Airways' main bases. This airline merged with North Central in 1979 to become Republic Airlines, which bought Hughes Airwest in October 1980. All were DC-9 operators, and the maintenance of these aircraft gravitated to Atlanta. When Northwest took over Republic in 1986, and its huge DC-9 fleet, it seemed logical to retain the Atlanta facility. Although Atlanta doesn't feature strongly in the current Northwest network, by careful rostering the airline manages to position aircraft to Atlanta for maintenance without having to fly 'dead-legs'.

Below: *Northwest Cargo Boeing 747-251F N629US (Fleet No 6729) is hardly recognisable behind access towers and platforms at Northwest's huge engineering facility at Minneapolis/St Paul, where over 2,300 engineers and technicians are employed.* Geoffrey P. Jones

Above: *A Northwest Boeing 747-251B undergoing a 'Heavy Overhaul' at the airline's engineering base at Minneapolis/St Paul where most work on the 747, DC-10 and 757 fleet is undertaken.* Geoffrey P. Jones

Duluth, on the western tip of Lake Superior, is Northwest's third big maintenance centre, built in 1989 specifically to deal with its Airbus A320 fleet. State help was provided in the financing of this important development, which has helped to regenerate the economy of this area. The facility here has been designed to accommodate the recent orders for further A320s and A319s, and A330s would also be maintained at Duluth. The eight Northwest MD-82s are also maintained at Duluth.

All Boeing 727 heavy maintenance is currently sub-contracted to private companies, Tramco at Everett, Washington State currently carrying out the majority of this work. Other heavy maintenance has to be out-sourced as well at times and throughout the world, so that KLM in Holland and FLS in Great Britain are used. Two other companies do some heavy maintenance work on the 'wide-body' fleet: SASCO in Singapore and TACO at Xhiamen in China.

Northwest takes an innovative approach to maintenance, splitting it into light, heavy and major categories (and so it is called the 'LHM' Programme). The airline chose this rather than the more traditional 'letter check' system of A, B, C and D checks, because of its airworthiness corrosion programme. This is type-specific rather than all-embracing.

As an example Northwest's Boeing 747 and DC-10 fleets have the following maintenance programme, with between 15- and 18-month intervals from 'major' to 'light':

- Major overhaul
- 2 x Light overhauls
- Heavy overhaul
- 2 x Light overhauls
- Major overhaul

Most of Northwest's equivalents to 'A' and 'B' checks are carried out on-line by the line maintenance mechanics. The 'A' equivalent is more detailed than the daily PS check and is performed roughly weekly, or every 60 hours flying time. The equivalent 'B' check is done approximately monthly, after between 300 to 500 hours flying time. Also on the long-haul fleets of 747 and DC-10 aircraft, Northwest carries out most of its equivalent to 'A' checks at one of Taipei, Tokyo (Narita) or Hong Kong.

Northwest Maintenance has been heavily involved in two programmes, integrated with the airline's fleet policy of refurbishing and retaining older aircraft, so long as they are safe, viable and practical. This applies to four main aircraft types, the DC-9, DC-10, Boeing 747-200 (Classics) and Boeing 727. Independent evaluations of the DC-9 airframe confirmed that it is one of the best constructed passenger aircraft ever. Before deciding on a refurbishment programme, Northwest engineers in conjunction with independent consultants confirmed that these aircraft would be safe for many years of additional flying. As a result, and bearing in mind the size of Northwest's DC-9 fleet (180 aircraft), the DC-9 refurbishment programme has become the airline's most significant.

At the Minneapolis/St Paul maintenance facility, under the direction of Dave Graham, the whole of the Northwest Airlines 747 'Classic' fleet is undergoing refurbishment in a two-year programme, with internal modifications and cabin refurbishment taking a priority. The DC-10 fleet is also scheduled for this treatment. One of the difficulties of such programmes is materials support, particularly with the older DC-9 and DC-10 variants. Manufacturers are no longer making many of the components and airframe parts for these aircraft, so Northwest has to manufacture many of them in-house or contract the work out.

External painting/spraying work on Northwest's entire fleet is also contracted out, particularly to KLM and to Leading Edge Inc of Greenville, Mississippi.

Most engine maintenance work is done at Northwest's main maintenance locations with representatives from Pratt & Whitney on site to help. Full engine test cells are located at Minneapolis/St Paul and Atlanta. The only engine work contracted out is on the CFM engines from the A320 fleet, maintained by KLM.

Left: *Northwest again led the US airline field with the January 1998 announcement that it had agreed a long-term commercial alliance with Houston-based Continental Airlines, including the acquisition of a 14% equity stake in Continental. Despite this alliance, the two airlines will not be merged.*
Geoffrey P. Jones

Left: *The magnitude of a Boeing 747 is often forgotten: ramp staff service Boeing 747-251B N614US at Minneapolis/St Paul and lend scale to this aircraft, one of the mainstays of Northwest's long-haul fleet.*
Geoffrey P. Jones

Below: *London Gatwick's satellite South Terminal is a hive of Northwest activity each morning with flights from Minneapolis/St Paul, Detroit and Boston. Two DC-10s and a Boeing 747 are seen at Gatwick in June 1995.*
Geoffrey P. Jones

Fleet List

(Correct to June 1998)

Airbus Industrie A320

Registration	Aircraft Type	Fleet No	Notes
N301US	A320-211	3201	ex-F-WWDJ
N302US	A320-211	3202	ex-F-WWDK
N303US	A320-211	3203	ex-F-WWDL
N304US	A320-211	3204	ex-F-WWDD
N305US	A320-211	3205	ex-F-WWDS
N306US	A320-211	3206	ex-F-WWIE
N307US	A320-211	3207	ex-F-WWIA
N308US	A320-211	3208	ex-F-WWIB
N309US	A320-211	3209	ex-F-WWIM
N310NW	A320-211	3210	ex-F-WWIO
N311US	A320-211	3211	ex-F-WWIT
N312US	A320-211	3212	ex-F-WWDT
N313US	A320-211	3213	ex-F-WWDX
N314US	A320-211	3214	ex-F-WWDZ
N315US	A320-211	3215	ex-F-WWIJ
N316US	A320-211	3216	ex-F-WWIY
N317US	A320-211	3217	ex-F-WWDF
N318US	A320-211	3218	ex-F-WWDK
N319US	A320-211	3219	ex-F-WWDT
N320US	A320-211	3220	ex-F-WWIB
N321US	A320-211	3221	ex-F-WWDI
N322US	A320-211	3222	ex-F-WWDQ
N323US	A320-211	3223	ex-F-WWBP
N324US	A320-211	3224	ex-F-WWDS
N325US	A320-211	3225	ex-F-WWBS
N326US	A320-211	3226	ex-F-WWIA
N327NW	A320-211	3227	ex-F-WWIO
N328NW	A320-211	3228	ex-F-WWIP
N329NW	A320-211	3229	ex-F-WWDG
N330NW	A320-211	3230	ex-F-WWDJ
N331NW	A320-211	3231	ex-F-WWBF
N332NW	A320-211	3232	ex-F-WWBG
N333NW	A320-211	3233	ex-F-WWDY
N334NW	A320-211	3234	ex-F-WWBP
N335NW	A320-211	3235	ex-F-WWBQ
N336NW	A320-211	3236	ex-F-WWIE
N337NW	A320-211	3237	ex-F-WWIO
N338NW	A320-211	3238	ex-F-WWBY
N339NW	A320-211	3239	ex-F-WWDG
N340NW	A320-211	3240	ex-F-WWIX
N341NW	A320-211	3241	ex-F-WWIS
N342NW	A320-211	3242	ex-F-WWIJ
N343NW	A320-211	3243	ex-F-WWBV
N344NW	A320-211	3244	ex-F-WWDC

N345NW	A320-211	3245	ex-F-WWIG	
N346NW	A320-211	3246	ex-F-WWII	
N347NW	A320-211	3247	ex-F-WWDN	
N348NW	A320-211	3248	ex-F-WWDV	
N349NW	A320-211	3249	ex-F-WWBR	
N350NW	A320-211	3250	ex-F-WWDG	
N351NW	A320-212	3251	ex-F-WWDG	delivered 27 Jan 1998
N352NW	A320-212	3252	ex-F-WWDO	delivered 24 Feb 1998
N353NW	A320-212	3253	ex-F-WWDP	delivered 13 Mar 1998
N354NW	A320-212	3254	ex-F-WWDY	delivered 21 April 1998
N355NW	A320-212	3255	ex-F-WWIC	delivered 24 April 1998
N356NW	A320-212	3256		
N357NW	A320-212		ex-F-WWIN	delivered June 1998
N358NW	A320-212		ex-F-WWIO	delivered June 1998
N359NW	A320-212		ex-F-WWBH	delivered July 1998
N360NW	A320-212			
N361NW	A320-212			
N362NW	A320-212			
N363NW	A320-212			
N364NW	A320-212			for delivery March 1999
N365NW	A320-212			for delivery March 1999
N366NW	A320-212			for delivery April 1999
N367NW	A320-212			for delivery April 1999

Three more due for delivery in 1999.
Fleet total — 70 aircraft, including 20 currently in delivery (N351NW onwards).

Airbus Industrie A330-300
All aircraft currently on order

Registration	Aircraft Type	Fleet No	Notes
N3301C	A330-321	3301	
N3302N	A330-321	3302	
N3303B	A330-321	3303	
N3304N	A330-321	3304	
N3305N	A330-321	3305	
N3306N	A330-321	3306	
N3307N	A330-321	3307	
N3308B	A330-321	3308	
N3309N	A330-321	3309	
N3310U	A330-321	3310	
N3311G	A330-321	3311	
N3312U	A330-321	3312	
N3313A	A330-321	3313	
N3314B	A330-321	3314	
N3315D	A330-321	3315	
N3316G	A330-321	3316	

Boeing 727-200 Series

Registration	Aircraft Type	Fleet No	Notes
N201US	B727-251	2201(H)	
N202US	B727-251	2202	
N203US	B727-251	2203	

Registration	Aircraft Type	Fleet No	Notes
N204US	B727-251	2204	
N275US	B727-251	2275	
N284US	B727-251	2284	
N285US	B727-251	2285	
N286US	B727-251	2286	
N287US	B727-251	2287	
N288US	B727-251	2288	
N289US	B727-251	2289	
N290US	B727-251	2290	
N291US	B727-251	2291	
N292US	B727-251	2292	
N293US	B727-251	2293	
N295US	B727-251	2295	
N296US	B727-251	2296	
N297US	B727-251	2297	
N298US	B727-251	2298	
N299US	B727-251	2299	
N712RC	B727-2S7	2712	ex-Republic Airlines
N715RC	B727-2S7	2711	ex-Republic Airlines
N716RC	B727-2S7	2713	ex-Republic Airlines
N718RC	B727-2S7	2714	ex-Republic Airlines
N719RC	B727-2S7	2715	ex-Republic Airlines
N720RC	B727-2S7	2716	ex-Republic Airlines
N721RC	B727-2S7	2717	ex-Republic Airlines
N722RW	B727-2M7	2762	ex-Hughes Airwest & Republic (with long-range tanks)
N727RW	B727-2M7	2767	ex-Hughes Airwest & Republic
N728RW	B727-2M7	2768	ex-Hughes Airwest & Republic
N729RW	B727-2M7	2769	ex-Hughes Airwest & Republic
N801EA	B727-225	2704	ex-Eastern Air Lines
N802EA	B727-225	2705	ex-Eastern Air Lines
N815EA	B727-225	2706	ex-Eastern Air Lines
N816EA*	B727-225	2707 (H)	ex-Eastern Air Lines
N817EA*	B727-225	2708 (H)	ex-Eastern Air Lines
N818EA*	B727-225	2709 (H)	ex-Eastern Air Lines
N820EA*	B727-225	2710	ex-Eastern Air Lines
N8877Z*	B727-225	2702	ex-Eastern Air Lines
N8878Z	B727-225	2703	ex-Eastern Air Lines

Boeing 727-200 Series fleet total — 40 aircraft.

* Aircraft which operate under a service agreement between Northwest and seven National Basketball Association teams and one National Hockey League team. Used during the teams' off season (summer) on regular commercial services.

(H) Hush-kitted

Boeing 747-200 Freighters

Registration	Aircraft Type	Fleet No	Notes
N616US	B747-251F	6716	
N617US	B747-251F	6717	
N618US	B747-251F	6718	
N619US	B747-251F	6719	
N629US	B747-251F	6729	

N630US	B747-2J9F	6730	ex-N1288E (ex-Boeing & Iranian AF)
N639US	B747-251F	6739	
N640US	B747-251F	6740	

Boeing 747-200 Freighter fleet — 8 aircraft (acquired between 1975 and 1987).
Note: N643NW, B747-249F and ex-9V-SQV was leased to Korean Air as HL7401 and then lease/purchased by Southern Air in Dec 1997 as N744SJ.

Boeing 747-100 and 200 Series

Registration	Aircraft Type	Fleet No	Notes
N601US	B747-151	6601	Now withdrawn from service
N603US	B747-151	6603	Now withdrawn from service
N608US	B747-151	6608	Now withdrawn from service
N611US	B747-251B	6611	
N612US	B747-251B	6612	
N613US	B747-251B	6613	
N614US	B747-251B	6614	
N615US	B747-251B	6615	
N622US	B747-251B	6622	
N623US	B747-251B	6623	
N624US	B747-251B	6624	
N625US	B747-251B	6625	
N626US	B747-251B	6626	
N627US	B747-251B	6627	
N628US	B747-251B	6628	
N631US	B747-251B	6631	
N632US	B747-251B	6632	
N633US	B747-227B	6633	ex-N8284V/N605BN Braniff
N634US	B747-227B	6634	ex-N1607B/N607BN Braniff
N635US	B747-227B	6635	ex-N602PE/N602BN Braniff
N636US	B747-251B	6636	
N637US	B747-251B	6637	
N638US	B747-251B	6638	
N641NW	B747-212B		ex-9V-SQP Singapore Airlines
N642NW	B747-212B		ex-9V-SQQ Singapore Airlines

Boeing 747-100 Series fleet total — 3 aircraft.
Boeing 747-200 Series fleet total — 22 aircraft.

Boeing 747-400 Series

Registration	Aircraft Type	Fleet No	Notes
N661US	B747-451	6301	ex-N401PW
N662US	B747-451	6302	ex-N302US
N663US	B747-451	6303	ex-N303US
N664US	B747-451	6304	ex-N304US Spirit of Beijing
N665US	B747-451	6305	ex-N305US
N666US	B747-451	6306	ex-N306US

Registration	Aircraft Type	Fleet No	Notes
N667US	B747-451	6307	ex-N307US
N668US	B747-451	6308	ex-N308US
N669US	B747-451	6309	ex-N309US
N670US	B747-451	6310	ex-N311US World Plane Colours

Boeing 747-400 Series fleet total — 10 aircraft.
Note: a further four B747-400s are on order.

Boeing 757-200 Series

Registration	Aircraft Type	Fleet No	Notes
N501US	B757-251	5501	City of St Paul
N502US	B757-251	5502	City of Minneapolis
N503US	B757-251	5503	City of Detroit
N504US	B757-251	5504	City of Los Angeles
N505US	B757-251	5505	City of Boston
N506US	B757-251	5506	City of New York
N507US	B757-251	5507	City of Seattle
N508US	B757-251	5508	City of Washington DC
N509US	B757-251	5509	City of Anchorage
N511US	B757-251	5511	City of Tampa
N512US	B757-251	5512	City of Chicago Bay
N513US	B757-251	5513	City of Orlando
N514US	B757-251	5514	City of San Francisco
N515US	B757-251	5515	City of Phoenix
N516US	B757-251	5516	City of San Diego
N517US	B757-251	5517	City of Portland
N518US	B757-251	5518	City of Milwaukee
N519US	B757-251	5519	City of Cleveland
N520US	B757-251	5520	City of Philadelphia
N521US	B757-251	5521	City of Denver
N522US	B757-251	5522	City of Spokane
N523US	B757-251	5523	City of Dallas
N524US	B757-251	5524	City of Houston
N525US	B757-251	5525	City of Miami
N526US	B757-251	5526	City of Memphis
N527US	B757-251	5527	City of Fargo
N528US	B757-251	5528	City of Toronto
N529US	B757-251	5529	City of New Orleans
N530US	B757-251	5530	City of Omaha
N531US	B757-251	5531	City of Newark
N532US	B757-251	5532	City of Fort Meyers
N533US	B757-251	5533	Cities of Orange County
N534US	B757-251	5534	City of Winnipeg
N535US	B757-251	5535	
N536US	B757-251	5536	
N537US	B757-251	5537	
N538US	B757-251	5538	
N539US	B757-251	5539	
N540US	B757-251	5540	
N541US	B757-251	5541	
N542US	B757-251	5542	

Registration	Aircraft Type	Fleet No	
N543US	B757-251	5543	
N544US	B757-251	5544	
N545US	B757-251	5545	
N546US	B757-251	5546	
N547US	B757-251	5547	
N548US	B757-251	5548	
N549US	B757-251	5549	

Boeing 757-200 fleet total — 48 aircraft.
Note: 25 further B757-251 aircraft are on order.

Douglas DC-9

Registration	Aircraft Type	Fleet No	Notes
N89S	DC-9-31	9930 (H)	
N90S	DC-9-31	9931 (H)	
N91S	DC-9-15	9101	
N92S	DC-9-15	9102	
N93S	DC-9-15	9103	
N94S	DC-9-15	9104	
N95S	DC-9-15	9105	
N96S	DC-9-15	9106	
N401EA	DC-9-51	9885	ex-N920VJ
N600TR	DC-9-51	9886	ex-YV-40C (long-range tanks)
N601NW	DC-9-32	9601 (H)	ex-I-DIBA
N602NW	DC-9-32	9602 (H)	ex-I-DIBE
N603NW	DC-9-32	9603 (H)	ex-I-DIBL
N604NW	DC-9-32	9604 (H)	ex-I-DIBP
N605NW	DC-9-32	9605 (H)	ex-I-DIBM
N606NW	DC-9-32	9606 (H)	ex-I-RIFG
N607NW	DC-9-32	9607 (H)	ex-I-RIFY
N608NW	DC-9-32	9608 (H)	ex-I-RIFC
N609NW	DC-9-32	9609 (H)	ex-I-RIFD
N610NW	DC-9-32	9610 (H)	ex-I-RIFB
N611NA	DC-9-32	9611 (H)	ex-I-RIFL
N612NW	DC-9-32	9612 (H)	ex-I-RIFZ
N613NW	DC-9-32	9613 (H)	ex-I-RIFP
N614NW	DC-9-32	9614 (H)	ex-I-RIFH
N615NW	DC-9-32	9615 (H)	ex-I-DIBI
N616NW	DC-9-32	9616 (H)	ex-I-RIFS
			Leased from May 1997
N617NW	DC-9-32	9617 (H)	ex-N911VV
N618NW	DC-9-32	9618 (H)	ex-I-RIFU
N619NW	DC-9-32	9619 (H)	ex-I-RIFE
N620NW	DC-9-32	9620	ex-I-RIFV
			Leased from July 1997
N621NW	DC-9-32	9621 (H)	ex-I-RIFM
N622NW	DC-9-32	9622	ex-I-RIFW
N623NW	DC-9-32	9623 (H)	ex-I-RIFT
N670MC	DC-9-51	9882	ex-HB-ISP
N671MC	DC-9-51	9883	ex-HB-ISR
N675MC	DC-9-51	9880	ex-OE-LDK
N676MC	DC-9-51	9881	ex-OE-LDL
N677MC	DC-9-51	9884	ex-OE-LDO

Registration	Type	MSN	Notes
N750NW	DC-9-41	9750	ex-SE-DBX
N751NW	DC-9-41	9751 (H)	ex-OY-KGA
N752NW	DC-9-41	9752	ex-LN-RLK
N753NW	DC-9-41	9753	ex-SE-DBW
N754NW	DC-9-41	9754	ex-OY-KGB
N755NW	DC-9-41	9755	ex-LN-RLC
N756NW	DC-9-41	9756 (H)	ex-SE-DBU
N758NW	DC-9-41	9758	ex-OY-KGC
N759NW	DC-9-41	9759	ex-LN-RLJ
N760NC	DC-9-51	9851	
N760NW	DC-9-41	9760	ex-SE-DBT
N761NC	DC-9-51	9852	
N762NC	DC-9-51	9853	
N762NW	DC-9-41	9762	ex-OY-KGG
N763NC	DC-9-51	9854	
N763NW	DC-9-41	9763 (H)	ex-LN-RLD
N764NC	DC-9-51	9855	
N765NC	DC-9-51	9856	
N766NC	DC-9-51	9857	
N767NC	DC-9-51	9858	
N768NC	DC-9-51	9859	
N769NC	DC-9-51	9860	
N770NC	DC-9-51	9861	
N771NC	DC-9-51	9862	
N772NC	DC-9-51	9863	
N773NC	DC-9-51	9864	
N774NC	DC-9-51	9865	
N775NC	DC-9-51	9866	Leased from GATX
N776NC	DC-9-51	9867	Leased from GATX
N777NC	DC-9-51	9868	Leased from GATX
N778NC	DC-9-51	9869	Leased from GATX
N779NC	DC-9-51	9870	Leased from GATX
N780NC	DC-9-51	9871	Leased from GATX
N781NC	DC-9-51	9872	
N782NC	DC-9-51	9873	
N783NC	DC-9-51	9874	
N784NC	DC-9-51	9875	
N785NC	DC-9-51	9876	
N786NC	DC-9-51	9877	
N787NC	DC-9-51	9878	
N908H	DC-9-31	9937 (H)	
N911RW	DC-9-31	9965 (H)	ex-N903H
N912RW	DC-9-31	9964 (H)	ex-N905H
N913RW	DC-9-31	9963 (H)	ex-N906H
N914RW	DC-9-31	9962 (H)	ex-N907H
N915RW	DC-9-31	9957	ex-N8930E
N916RW	DC-9-31	9952 (H)	ex-N8935E
N917RW	DC-9-31	9958	ex-N8936E
N918RW	DC-9-31	9953	ex-N8937E
N919RW	DC-9-31	9959 (H)	ex-N8939E
N920RW	DC-9-31	9960 (H)	ex-N8940E
N921RW	DC-9-31	9954	ex-N8941E
N922RW	DC-9-31	9955	ex-N8946E

N923RW	DC-9-31	9956	ex-N8947E
N924RW	DC-9-31	9961 (H)	ex-N8949E
N925US	DC-9-32	9925 (H)	ex-YU-AHO
N926NW	DC-9-32	9926	ex-YU-AHL
N926RC	DC-9-32	9924	ex-YU-AHP
N927RC	DC-9-32	9923 (H)	ex-YU-AHM
N930RC	DC-9-15	9140	ex-OH-LYE
N940N	DC-9-32	9918	
N941N	DC-9-32	9919	ex-D-ADIT
N942N	DC-9-32	9920	ex-D-ADIS
N943N	DC-9-32	9921	
N945N	DC-9-32	9922	
N948L	DC-9-14	9139	ex-N6140A
N949N	DC-9-32	9916	
N952N	DC-9-31	9902 (H)	
N953N	DC-9-31	9903 (H)	
N955N	DC-9-31	9905 (H)	
N956N	DC-9-31	9906 (H)	
N957N	DC-9-31	9907 (H)	
N958N	DC-9-31	9908 (H)	
N959N	DC-9-31	9909 (H)	
N960N	DC-9-31	9910 (H)	
N961N	DC-9-31	9911 (H)	
N962N	DC-9-31	9912 (H)	
N963N	DC-9-31	9913 (H)	
N964N	DC-9-31	9914 (H)	
N965N	DC-9-31	9915 (H)	
N967N	DC-9-32	9917	
N982US	DC-9-32	9982	ex-HB-IFH
N983US	DC-9-32	9983	ex-HB-IFU
N984US	DC-9-32	9984	ex-HB-IFV
N985US	DC-9-32	9985	ex-HB-IFZ
N986US	DC-9-32	9986	ex-N988US
N987US	DC-9-32	9987	ex-OE-LDF
N994Z	DC-9-31	9981 (H)	ex-N979NE
N1308T	DC-9-31	9943 (H)	
N1309T	DC-9-31	9944 (H)	
N1332U	DC-9-31	9935 (H)	
N1334U	DC-9-31	9933 (H)	
N1798U	DC-9-31	9938 (H)	
N1799U	DC-9-31	9936 (H)	
N3310L	DC-9-14	9178	
N3322L	DC-9-32	9940 (H)	ex-YV-68C
N3324L	DC-9-32	9941 (H)	ex-YV-70C
N3991C	DC-9-32	9942	ex-PJ-SNE
N8906E	DC-9-14	9163	
N8907E	DC-9-14	9162	
N8908E	DC-9-14	9150	ex-N90588
N8909E	DC-9-14	9151 (H)	
N8911E	DC-9-14	9152	
N8912E	DC-9-14	9153	
N8913E	DC-9-14	9154	
N8914E	DC-9-14	9155	

N8915E	DC-9-14	9156	
N8920E	DC-9-31	9927 (H)	
N8921E	DC-9-31	9928 (H)	
N8923E	DC-9-31	9929 (H)	
N8925E	DC-9-31	9945 (H)	
N8926E	DC-9-31	9946 (H)	
N8928E	DC-9-31	9949 (H)	
N8929E	DC-9-31	9948 (H)	
N8932E	DC-9-31	9996 (H)	
N8933E	DC-9-31	9997 (H)	
N8934E	DC-9-31	9998 (H)	
N8938E	DC-9-31	9947 (H)	ex-5N-GIN
N8944E	DC-9-31	9988 (H)	
N8945E	DC-9-31	9989 (H)	
N8950E	DC-9-31	9990 (H)	ex-C-FBKT
N8957E	DC-9-31	9991 (H)	
N8960E	DC-9-31	9992 (H)	
N8978E	DC-9-31	9995 (H)	
N8979E	DC-9-31	9994 (H)	
N8986E	DC-9-31	9993 (H)	ex-5N-INZ
N9330	DC-9-31	9966 (H)	ex-N9105
N9331	DC-9-31	9967 (H)	
N9332	DC-9-31	9968 (H)	
N9333	DC-9-31	9969 (H)	
N9334	DC-9-31	9970	
N9335	DC-9-31	9971 (H)	
N9336	DC-9-31	9972 (H)	
N9337	DC-9-31	9973 (H)	
N9338	DC-9-31	9974 (H)	
N9339	DC-9-31	9975 (H)	
N9340	DC-9-31	9976 (H)	
N9341	DC-9-31	9977 (H)	
N9342	DC-9-31	9978 (H)	
N9343	DC-9-31	9979 (H)	
N9344	DC-9-31	9980 (H)	
N9346	DC-9-32	9950 (H)	ex-N394PA
N9347	DC-9-32	9951(H)	ex-HL7201
N9348	DC-9-15	9138	ex-N1793U
N12532	DC-9-32		ex-N532TX

Douglas DC-9 fleet total (all variants) — 181 aircraft.
(H) — denotes hush-kitted engines fitted.

McDonnell Douglas MD-82

N301RC	MD-82	9301	
N302RC	MD-82	9302	
N307RC	MD-82	9305	
N309RC	MD-82	9307	ex-N10045
N311RC	MD-82	9308	ex-N1004D
N313RC	MD-82	9310	ex-N1004G
N314RC	MD-82	9311	ex-N1004L
N931MC	MD-82	9304	ex-N10035

McDonnell Douglas MD-82 fleet total — 8 aircraft.

McDonnell Douglas DC-10

Registration	Aircraft Type	Fleet No	Notes
N133JC	DC-10-40	1143	ex-N143US
N141US	DC-10-40	1141	
N144JC	DC-10-40	1144	ex-N144US Leased from Sun Country
N145US	DC-10-40	1145	
N146US	DC-10-40	1146	
N147US	DC-10-40	1147	
N148US	DC-10-40	1148	
N149US	DC-10-40	1149	
N150US	DC-10-40	1150	
N151US	DC-10-40	1151	
N152US	DC-10-40	1152	
N153US	DC-10-40	1153	
N154US	DC-10-40	1154	
N155US	DC-10-40	1155	
N156US	DC-10-40	1156	
N157US	DC-10-40	1157	
N158US	DC-10-40	1158	
N159US	DC-10-40	1159	
N160US	DC-10-40	1160	
N161US	DC-10-40	1161	
N162US	DC-10-40	1162	
N211NW	DC-10-30	1211	ex-HB-IHP Leased from Electra
N220NW	DC-10-30	1220	ex-HB-IHC
N221NW	DC-10-30	1221	ex-HB-IHE
N223NW	DC-10-30	1223	ex-HB-IHF
N224NW	DC-10-30	1224	ex-HB-IHG
N225NW	DC-10-30	1225	ex-HB-IHH
N226NW	DC-10-30ER	1226	ex-HB-IHL
N227NW	DC-10-30	1227	ex-HB-IHI
N228NW	DC-10-30	1228	
N229NW	DC-10-30	1229	ex-N4655Y
N230NW	DC-10-30	1230	ex-N4655Z
N232NW	DC-10-30	1232	ex-N961GF
N233NW	DC-10-30	1233	ex-N962GF
N234NW	DC-10-30	1234	ex-HL7316
N235NW	DC-10-30	1235	ex-HL7317
N236NW	DC-10-30	1236	ex-HL7315
N237NW	DC-10-30	1237	ex-PP-VMW Purchased Dec 1997
N238NW	DC-10-30	1238	ex-HS-TMA
N239NW	DC-10-30	1239	ex-HS-TMB
N240NW	DC-10-30	1240	ex-HS-TMC

McDonnell Douglas DC-10 fleet total — 41 aircraft.

The UK's fastest growing aviation magazine...

Aircraft ILLUSTRATED

- **INCORPORATING —**
  Air Display International
- **BIGGER, BUMPER ISSUES —**
  96 pages of solid aviation
- **UNBEATABLE COVERAGE —**
  of the aviation scene – military, civil, past and present
- **STUNNING IMAGES —**
  from the top aviation photographers, including many *exclusives* from JOHN DIBBS
- **UNRIVALLED COVERAGE —**
  of the airshow scene – news, previews, interviews, 'in cockpit' reports and much more

Subscribe today to <u>THE</u> magazine for the aviation enthusiast.

For details of subscriptions please contact:
Subscriptions Department, Ian Allan Publishing Ltd, Riverdene Business Park, Molesey Road, Hersham, Surrey KT12 4RG.
Tel: 01932 266622   Fax: 01932 266633

Be assured of your copy by ordering now!